THE ROYAL
NAVY IN THE
NAPOLEONIC AGE

For two women who inspire me: Wendy, for her spitfire spirit; and Jen, for her fortitude.

THE ROYAL NAVY IN THE NAPOLEONIC AGE

SENIOR SERVICE, 1800–1815

Mark Jessop

PEN & SWORD **HISTORY**

AN IMPRINT OF PEN & SWORD BOOKS LTD.
YORKSHIRE – PHILADELPHIA

First published in Great Britain in 2019 by
PEN AND SWORD HISTORY
an imprint of
Pen and Sword Books Ltd
Yorkshire – Philadelphia

Copyright © Mark Jessop, 2019

ISBN 978 1 52672 037 5

Printed and bound in the UK
by TJ International, Padstow, Cornwall, PL28 8RW

Typeset in Times New Roman 11/13.5 by
Aura Technology and Software Services, India

Pen & Sword Books Ltd incorporates the imprints of Pen & Sword
Archaeology, Atlas, Aviation, Battleground, Discovery,
Family History, History, Maritime, Military, Naval, Politics, Railways,
Select, Social History, Transport, True Crime, Claymore Press,
Frontline Books, Leo Cooper, Praetorian Press, Remember When,
Seaforth Publishing and Wharncliffe.

For a complete list of Pen and Sword titles please contact
Pen and Sword Books Limited
47 Church Street, Barnsley, South Yorkshire, S70 2AS, England
E-mail: enquiries@pen-and-sword.co.uk
Website: www.pen-and-sword.co.uk

Or

PEN AND SWORD BOOKS
1950 Lawrence Rd, Havertown, PA 19083, USA
E-mail: Uspen-and-sword@casematepublishers.com
Website: www.penandswordbooks.com

Contents

Preface

In 1801 the United Kingdom of Great Britain and Ireland commenced the nineteenth century as a nation at war. Its new imperial parliament[1] opened by commission on 22 January 1801, and by the king on 2 February 1801. The new flag sported the red saltire of Ireland. The process required to create it had been prolonged and painful. Although her enemies failed to ruin her sea commerce, hardships had been inflicted. Food prices climbed and men and women were bone weary of hostilities. The threat of invasion and insurrection ran high.

Napoléon Bonaparte was no ordinary opponent. His move to secure northern Italy, and the Battle of Marengo demonstrated his resolve. But his success was on land. At sea it remained a different matter. What stood in his way was the Royal Navy. To divert attention away from his invasion of England, Napoléon looked north towards the Baltic. Another theatre of war was added to those already covered by British warships.

The United Kingdom boasted a number of superb ports and naval yards. Portsmouth was the main naval arsenal but there were others. Commonly referred to as 'Plymouth', this West Country town comprised three separate conurbations: Plymouth, East Stonehouse and Dock. At Dock the Royal Navy maintained a large and vibrant shipyard. Commenced after the civil war, it had begun to form a respectable sized town by 1730.[2] In succeeding years, with wars against America and revolutionary France, she almost doubled in size and population to become the 'Second Port of the Kingdom'.[3] Dock was more than capable of accommodating a fleet in a basin of the Tamar, called the Hamoaze, but that was up river and to get there vessels had to navigate the Sound which was open to gales and other navigational hazards, so the Navy had had to develop other anchorages along the coast.

---

1 Bigland, 1815, 483.

2 Hoxland, 1796, 5

3 Hoxland, *ibid*, 3

What kept Britain safe was her warships, the wooden wall that comprised her oldest continual military force. Although not the only means they were the first line of defence. The ships of the Royal Navy defended the United Kingdom and projected British force around the globe. The Royal Navy was the senior service.

Note

The events mentioned in this book are based on fact and those named naval officers, politicians and Frenchmen were actual people. However, to represent the men and women swept up in the tide of history, often unknown and unnamed, the characters who recount their memories and thoughts within are fictitious; such as the Danish pilot, the German gentleman, the canting crew, the nurse, the petty officers and three sisters, the poet, lieutenant, abolitionist, the chaplain and fellow survivors, the invalid, the man of North Riding, Zoilus and Taunton, the diarist, widow, the Madras man, captain, boatman and the judge.

Major Events Between 1801 and 1815

1801:

9 February. The Treaty of Lunéville (between France and Austria) effectively isolated the United Kingdom.

16 February. Prime Minister Pitt suddenly resigned.

8 March. Admiral Lord Keith's fleet landed troops at Aboukir. Commodore Sir Sidney Smith commanded the marines and seamen.

2 April. The Battle of Copenhagen.

2 September. British naval and military forces captured Alexandria.

1 October. A preliminary peace treaty was made.

1802:

27 March. Peace signed between the United Kingdom, France, Spain and the Batavian Republic.

29 April. Marines renamed 'Royal Marines'.

29 December. The British government instigated an enquiry into embezzlement and fraud in naval yards, and prize money.

1803:

30 January. An infamous report by Colonel Horace François Bastien Sébastiani de La Porta appeared in the *Moniteur*.

8 March. Public message issued by King George III.

18 May. Britain declared war on France.

Block mills built at Portsmouth.

1804:

15 March. William Pitt attacked Earl St Vincent over the readiness of the fleet.

12 December. Spain declared war against Britain.

1805:

30 March to 18 August. French warships cruised from Cadiz to the West Indies without meeting the British.

9 August. Austria joined Britain and Russian alliance to form the Third Coalition.

24 August. The Boulogne invasion camp began to break up.

21 October. The Battle of Trafalgar.

1806:

Trial of Henry Dundas.

21 November. The Berlin Decree was issued to commence the 'Continental System', a complete embargo of British goods.

1807:

7 January. An Order in Council was issued regarding seizure of neutral vessels.

25 March. An Act for the Abolition of the Slave Trade was decreed.

July - September. 'Violation' of Denmark by the Royal Navy.

11 November. An Order in Council was issued which prohibited direct trade to places in Europe where the United Kingdom was excluded.

17 December. France made the Decree of Milan which ordered the blockade of Britain.

1808:

25 June. HMS *Caledonia* (120), then the world's largest ship, was launched at Plymouth.

August. Britain gained a foothold in Portugal.

Royal Navy West Africa Squadron was formed to prevent the African slave trade.

1809:

Princetown Prison, Dartmoor, was built to hold prisoners.

1810:

19 June. HMS *Minden* (74), built of teak, was launched at Bombay.

1811:

14 May. The Slave Trade Felony Act was passed.

MAJOR EVENTS BETWEEN 1801 AND 1815

1812:

18 June. The United States of America declared war on the United Kingdom.

12 August. Work commenced on the Plymouth breakwater.

1813:

18 February. George Canning made a speech to parliament on rights of search and how the Royal Navy had lost its spell of invincibility.

3 April. Boats cut out schooners in the Rappahannock.

1814:

11 April. End of the Continental System.

24 August. A British force burned the White House.

1815:

15 July. Bonaparte surrendered to the British.

27 July. Bonaparte on show in Plymouth Sound onboard HMS *Bellerophon*.

7 August. Bonaparte left the sound and sailed into exile.

Chapter 1

But Work their Woe, and thy Renown

Boom! Boom! Boom!

Less than a cable length[4] away more than twenty angry cannons were aimed their way. Although dismasted their foe had once been a 48 and still appeared dangerous. 'They're certainly stubborn,' opined a small, ruddy faced midshipman all puffed up with importance. 'And the shore batteries have hot shot.' The taller pilot who stood beside him nodded agreement but the lad was too excited to notice. Deep in thought the older man wondered if the youngster, a veritable bantam, realized he was himself a Dansker.[5] Did the midshipman think he served as pilot because he had only studied some charts? Did he not notice his accent?

At the binnacle of HMS *Edgar,* her guns at play against the moored enemy hulk, the pilot looked with fondness towards the splitflag flying over the Danish ship. More so with the Dannebrog rød, the national flag, high over the blue-grey roofs of the arsenal. The smoke-shrouded spires of Copenhagen, his old home, stood two points off their larboard bow. With every salvo sent their way he felt both pride and terror. Now a resident of Norfolk it would be sadly ironic if a Danish ball were to end his days.

'I do believe,' continued the young gentleman, 'we will witness some long hot work, but I am very positive we will prevail. Lord Nelson will see to that.'

He found the youngster's enthusiasm amusing but quietly agreed the vice admiral would secure victory. After all he was the Hero of the Nile, had never yet suffered a defeat.

---

4 Homans, 1859, 1945. A cable is one tenth of a sea mile or roughly 120 fathoms, 240 yards or 720 feet.

5 A Dane, as found in Hamlet Act II, Scene I where Polonius says, *'Look you, sir, Inquire me first what Danskers are in Paris'.*

The Dane observed everything yet remained remote. A retired master of small merchant vessels he was no fighting man. His hair was as white as his courage. He hated every report of the great guns and their noise was a torture that made his tinnitus worse.[6] Although he stood amidst a small group of master, masters' mates and the midshipman, he had never felt so lonely his entire life. This was no place to be standing, and the British and Danes were doing as much damage to each other as they could!

Boom! Boom! Boom!

The older man had boarded the *Edgar* while she lay off Yarmouth, part of a fifty-three sail fleet set to foray deep into the Baltic. He was one of two dozen, mostly British born, licensed pilots who knew that sea well. The Baltic powers' resentments over the rights of their shipping had occasioned a northern League of Armed Neutrality – Russia, Sweden, Prussia and Denmark-Norway. Before they had sailed the ship's first lieutenant stated to gathered midshipmen that Denmark would receive notice to secede from the alliance, and when no longer a threat the fleet would continue eastwards to deal with the Russians at Revel.[7] He had stood to one side, a quiet civilian guest, but he recognised the wisdom of moving *before winter ice thawed* in the east. It had been a mild winter.

They sailed on 12 March 1801 and a week later, despite a severe snowstorm off Norway, reached the Kattegat to anchor north of the three mile wide strait that separates Denmark and Sweden. The midshipman realized the ship's youngsters had no idea of the geography of either Denmark or the Baltic. Such things were concerns for more experienced officers.

Boom! Boom! Boom!

Good God! The noise! He appeared calm on the surface but with every report of the guns fell deeper into a blue funk. When a Danish ball flew by he involuntarily raised his right hand in alarm and nearly hit the youngster in the face. He had to mask his anguish by flicking back his hair. To take his mind off the ordeal he tried to think through recent events.

They had loitered for days in the Kattegat. People wondered whether there would be peace? The tall spire of Kronborg castle, known as Elsinore by the British, captivated everyone, but they remained safely out of reach of her battery. Discussions with the ship's master centered on possible

---

6 Lake, 1805, 42. Tinnitus was discussed in numerous 18th/early 19th century books.

7 Or Reval. Now called Tallinn (Estonia). Nelson wanted to attack the Russian fleet first, before the British fleet was weakened by the Danes. See Mahan, 1902, 75. Revel held at least half of the Russian Baltic fleet.

directions they might approach Copenhagen – by way of the Great Belt, or directly through the Sound?

Boom! Boom! Boom!

When representatives repaired on board the flagship all flag officers had convened in the Admiral's Grand Cabin. It did not take long for news to spread that the Danish Crown Prince had refused to negotiate. So the fleet admiral sent a note to Kronborg asking whether they would fire as they made their way into the Sound and the reply had been all too obvious. A show was made after they weighed but the fleet hugged the Swedish shore and remained out of reach. The pilot heard someone ask why Swedish batteries remained quiet, but he had been too busy navigating through the shallows and sandbars to worry. They anchored off Hven island, with her famous low observatories built by Tycho Brahe, and Copenhagen then lay but fifteen miles over the horizon.

Boom! Boom! Boom!

An anxious council of war[8] followed in which Nelson argued for prompt action before a Swedish fleet could intervene, although he considered the combined fleets no match for the British. Not every naval officer then present concurred. The general consensus was that whereas most Danish ships would prove to be unserviceable the British delay would allow Danish defences to be strengthened. Two artificial island forts protected the entrance to the inner harbour, of which the larger, Trekroner (three-crown) Battery, commanded heavy cannon. A chain would have been placed across the harbour as a further hindrance and hulks moored close to shore in support of land batteries.

There were therefore but two options to land their troops: either a direct assault on the harbour, or a longer dogleg approach down the Outer Channel to Draco Point then up the King's Deep directly in front of Copenhagen and the entrance to the harbour. This longer, more difficult, passage required navigation of shoal waters of the Middelgrund but did permit an easier approach from the weaker southeastern direction. Both options required ships of shallow draft and Nelson offered to lead the attack with ten sail of the line. His offer was readily accepted and he received twelve sail of the line to do so. He would command from the *Elephant* (74)[9] with Rear Admiral Graves present onboard the *Defiance* (74). Admiral Parker would command the remainder of the fleet in deeper waters to guard against any Swedish intervention.

---

8 Massey, 1865, 349. His words.

9 James, Vol III, 96.

Nelson then gathered some officers, took a boat and for two days reconnoitered the first part of the approach. Normal buoys had been tampered with, even removed, and there was the risk of deliberately submerged dangers. So they placed their own buoys. The Outer Channel it would be.

Boom! Boom! Boom!

On 1 April 1801 more than thirty British warships had gotten under weigh. The Danish pilot was impressed when ships' complements shouted raucous joy throughout the division. As they entered the Outer Channel he clearly saw Copenhagen's fearsome fixed batteries and a mile-long line of ordnance moored in front.[10] One seaman was heard to tell another, *Look mate, see how they have a-sunk block-ships to hinder us? See those rafts? Radeaus they're called. Ra-deaus! Is you deaf? An those flat-bottomed boats are praams. Count 'em, but I reckon there be 600 Danish guns. All of them will be aimed at your ugly mug. Ha ha, see if they ain't!* And the midshipman pointed out two 70s and a large frigate within the inner road.[11]

Finally off Draco Point the wind was found to be against them so they had anchored, to pass the evening and cold night in anxious expectation of the next morning. The pilot chose to remain on deck and was given the courtesy of a chair and large blanket.

Early the next morning the excitement built. Men were distracted. Everyone wondered whether the wind would turn in their favour. Captain Murray repaired to the flagship to receive his allotted station, and on his return it was announced the *Edgar* was chosen to lead the way and anchor opposite the fifth enemy hulk in the Danish line. No one seemed to know her name but the pilot thought she might be the *Jylland*. He took a deep breath, for the hulk was large. It bristled with guns. When asked for his opinions upon dangers of shoalwater thereabouts his comments had been noted down and taken to Nelson with all other pilots' thoughts. They waited. Just after nine o'clock, the wind turned and the signal was hoisted to weigh. When the master[12] of the *Bellona* appeared on their quarterdeck to help lead the division the old pilot and ship's master had not felt any affront. They understood the importance of *Edgar*'s role and what she meant for British success.

Boom! Boom! Boom!

---

10 Shippen, 1894, 365. Nelson later reported the Danish line to consist of 'six sail of the line, eleven floating batteries, mounting from twenty-six 24-pounders, to eighteen 18-pounders, and one bomb-ship, besides schooner gun vessels'. See also Robinson, 1801, under 'COP'.

11 Bisset, 1803, 409.

12 Mr Briarly. See James, *ibid*, 117.

The *Edgar* eventually anchored by the stern opposite that fifth enemy hulk. Like all others of the British division her prow faced north, while the Danes' prows faced south. The remainder of the division made their way to anchor opposite their own designated hulks and floating batteries, or moved up as far as the Trekroner Battery and the nearby star fortress.[13] However, two British ships managed to run aground and one failed to weather the turn. One of the two that grounded happened to be the *Bellona* which must have truly mortified her master. Their combined loss seriously weakened the division but the frigates managed to fill the gap and the bomb ships anchored near the Middelgrund.

As shot hit the ship, the pilot wondered whether his fellow pilots could have done any better? He knew some had only worked small vessels, much like himself, and had no experience with large and cumbersome warships. He sensed that some sailors considered the pilots could not be trusted and a few had even given him dark and menacing looks.[14]

Boom! Boom! Boom!

So here they lay, motionless, with the noise now tedious. It was either their own guns, the thrum of enemy shot and the drone of balls, or the sickening thud meaning damage and injury. Their weather deck was a black and red shambles of ruined rigging, tattered canvas, splintered wood and pools of blood. Sailors had to clear away the debris and their curses were colourful. But the Danes suffered worse. One hulk, four ahead in their line, burned bright[15] and the pilot could see how Danish troops and sailors had tired. British boats, full of seamen and troops of the 49th regiment, plied the waters between, intent on boarding the enemy. Some were fired upon. When a master's mate ran past and said, 'The *Isis* is taking a cruel beating,' the pilot received a knowing look from the midshipman. The youth's response was to assume a remote professional visage, one he had seen his captain make, while the older man clenched his jaw.

Despite superior British gunnery, and seizure of some Danish ships, the battle reached an exhausted impasse. The fleet admiral had ordered them to retreat – the signal flew at his masthead – and while a few ships obeyed, Nelson had not. Perhaps the vice admiral could see what the fleet admiral could not? Most of the division, including the *Edgar*, continued to fire.

Boom! Boom! Boom!

---

13 Frederikshavn, or the Kastellet.

14 Nelson did not place any blame on those captains of grounded ships, nor apparently their pilots.

15 The flagship, *Dannebrog*.

A rough looking messenger came onboard with sad news about Captain Riou of the *Amazon*. 'Damn me,' he reported, 'but there he sat with a splinter wound to his head, marines lying all around him; he said "What will Nelson think of us?"[16], stood up to take the mainbrace, and a shot cut him clean in two.' The old man's face drained of colour. After that he paid no further attention to the noise and course of battle but stood alone in dark reverie.

Through a mist of melancholy and dull ringing in his ears he was told in snippets how Nelson sent a letter of truce ashore, that the boat which carried it had had to make a long pull to the inner harbour and a Danish boat under its own flag of truce had approached the *Elephant* with a reply. By mid-afternoon the battle was over.

The pilot observed the extent of destruction. Ahead in the distance the Trekroner fort and battery appeared little damaged while all of the Danish hulks to the south either floated adrift or were taken. It was a sorry sight. As for the British their ships had been terribly mauled, especially the *Defiance*, and most needed repairs. The wind was fair to allow them to depart but the division would have to pass under the gaze of that fierce Trekroner battery and three of their ships remained aground. Time would be needed to refloat them. When news reached them that Nelson had repaired ashore for negotiations the pilot took that to mean that the vice admiral was intent on gaining them time.

A commotion up front was soon explained to be a message trumpeted from the *Ardent*. A fourteen week armistice had been agreed. Fourteen weeks! Plenty of time. Fatigued as they were the ship's complement immediately gained a second wind and took to repairs to be ready for departure. The galley stove was fired up and grog handed out. The pilot downed his glass with relish while he listened to the master inform him they were headed for Sweden. He dumbly nodded his thanks but silently hoped that further conflict would be avoided. Perhaps Sweden and Russia would now seek peace? Visions of a small cottage on the Norfolk Broads, a certificate for payment safely in his pocket and an end to all this stuff and nonsense were his main concerns. The dull ache in his ears proclaimed that war was not for him.

Before Copenhagen, Denmark-Norway and Sweden had become disgruntled with British insistence on searching their merchantmen for goods, ammunition and naval stores that might be used by France and her allies. Denmark had complained to London about a series of hostile

---

16 Barker, 1836, 122. The *Amazon* frigate had turned her stern towards the Trekroner battery.

encounters at sea – there had been an issue involving a Danish frigate in 1800 – but Britain insisted she would continue to search any neutral ship 'steering towards the enemy's country'.[17] Sweden and Denmark could not then force the issue and had to persevere, but the situation radically changed after Bonaparte offered Russia possession of Malta.

Through the late summer of 1800, and into the following winter months, the Russians had seized British 'ships in Russian ports, and almost compelled Prussia to join the Armed Neutrality League'.[18] Prussia, swayed by so many angry nations around her, could not help but join. Her involvement threatened Baltic supplies of spars and masts for the Royal Navy and opened up British estates in Germany to seizure. A united Baltic fleet threatened Britain's east coast.

The northern league formed as Great Britain passed away to become the United Kingdom of Great Britain and Ireland. Her first parliament met on 2 January 1801 and within five weeks received news of the Treaty of Lunéville. It was 'based on the Treaty of Campo Formio... an agreement between France and Austria, constituting the Rhine a boundary for the eastern frontier of France'.[19] The United Kingdom stood alone and she had much to lose. Her imports and exports exceeded £70,000,000,[20] and it was these that allowed her to wage an expensive war. Her interests had to be protected.

The Royal Navy long protected the British Isles and her colonies. Her fleets had grown substantially since war broke out in 1793. Abstracts for the year 1801 laid out how 452 ships were then in commission with 39 ships in ordinary. Combined with harbour ships, ships ordered or building the grand total came to 771 ships and vessels. This force was deemed the senior British armed service not for her size, effectiveness and renown (the British army had its own prestige) but because she was the oldest continual armed force parliament commanded. Government policy, funding and voted estimates for manpower had created a true Neptune, a naval superpower. Pitt said, 'the naval preponderance which we have... acquired, has given security to this country, and has more than once afforded chances for the salvation of Europe'.[21]

The entrance by the British fleet into the Baltic, then little known to most of her officers and masters, added to the renown of Nelson. Together

---

17 Bissett, *ibid*, 723.

18 Rose, 1834, 129. It was signed on 16 December 1800.

19 Burnham, 1891, 744.

20 Mahan, *ibid*, 18. He reckoned it to be £73,000,000.

21 Debrett, 1801, 57.

with earlier landings in Egypt by Admiral Keith it buffed the lustre of the Royal Navy all the brighter. The French navy had been mostly bottled up in Brest and Toulon and had only managed to put forth when the blockading British had been blown off station by heavy weather. The French tried to bring about a 'final great design',[22] a united force of French and allied ships, but that hope remained unfulfilled. With captures taken at Copenhagen, the Royal Navy increased further throughout 1801.[23]

However, national exhaustion had set in. In February 1801 'Mr Pitt had given in his resignation followed by that of Lord Grenville, Earl Spencer, the Lord Chancellor, Mr. Dundas, and Mr. Windham, - ministers who had long enjoyed the confidence of the nation.'[24] Pitt may have resigned because he foresaw difficulties of 'financial arrangements requisite for a protracted war', his position would only deter a peace, and he had failed to emancipate Catholics;[25] but he believed Britain had achieved her main aim of 'security'.

The timing of the change was particularly problematic. A whole new government had to be formed just as King George III was 'seized with an indisposition',[26] a euphemism for madness. Viscount Sidmouth took the treasury, Lord Eldon lord high chancellor, Colonel Yorke secretary of war and Earl St Vincent first lord of the admiralty. Of their initial priorities they needed to confront the northern league. Thus, the British fleet that formed at Yarmouth.

Nelson's division comprised: the 74s *Bellona, Defiance, Edgar* (Captain George Murray), *Elephant* (Vice Admiral Nelson), *Ganges, Monarch* and *Russell;* the 64s *Agamemnon, Ardent* and *Polyphemus*; the 50s *Glatton and Isis; Amazon* (38); the 36s *Blanche* and *Desiree*; *Alcmene* (32); *Dart* (28); *Jamaica* (24); *Arrow* (20); the 18s *Cruizer* and *Harpy*; bombs and fireships. The reserve was made up of the 98s *London* (Admiral Hyde Parker) and *St George*; the 74s *Defence, Ramillies, Saturn* and *Warrior*; and the 64s *Raisonnable* and *Veteran* .

They arrived off Denmark in support of the British representative Nicholas Vansittart and William Drummond, the chargé d'affaires at Copenhagen. Those two men hoped peace would be concluded if Denmark abandoned the league, desisted from using convoys, allowed British searches of Danish merchantmen and gave free passage to British ships through their sound.

---

22 Mahan's words, *ibid*, 63.

23 *Abstracts of the British Navy.*

24 Bigland, 1815, 481.

25 Bigland, *ibid.*

26 Bigland, *ibid*, 482.

Opposed to them was the armed league. The Russians had thirty-one sail in commission in the Baltic (but only twenty serviceable), Sweden had eleven sail of the line and Denmark ten sail of the line fit for service. Such numbers were unlikely to combine in one force against the British.[27]

The consequent Battle of Copenhagen, which the Danes call *Slaget på Reden*, brought ruination upon eighteen Danish ships and 'about two thousand of their bravest seamen'.[28]

It became famous for what Nelson did and did not do. When the signal to break off was hoisted he was reported to have ignored it: "'Leave off action! Now damn me if I do! You know, Foley,' turning to the captain, 'I have only one eye - I have a right to be blind sometimes:' - and then putting the glass to his blind eye, in that mood which sports with bitterness, he exclaimed, 'I really do not see the signal!'"[29] The debate ever since has been whether Admiral Hyde Parker opted to allow Nelson to retreat and save face. At the time the signal was hoisted, the British squadron appeared to be taking a serious beating. The battle demonstrated Danish courage and discipline. Parker supposedly said, 'If Nelson is in a condition to continue the action he will disregard it; if he is not, it will be an excuse for his retreat.'[30]

Copenhagen also highlighted the British fleets' regular use of pilots. Masters normally served as pilots in the Navy with charge of the ship's steerage during a voyage, and in battle could give advice, but his captain's orders always superseded him. In most circumstances the master took control of the ship's navigation and was accountable for such, but sometimes a warship required a licensed pilot to come onboard. The *Regulations and Instructions Relating to His Majesty's Service at Sea* had laid out how a pilot might take command of a warship, giving 'Orders for steering, setting, or handling Sails, bracing the Yards, putting the Ship at Stays, or any other Acts that concern the navigation of the Ship'.[31] The regulations implied much suspicion. The captain was expected to attend to the pilot's conduct and ability at all times and if any doubts were raised the pilot had to be dismissed. For the captain was always in charge and was expected to keep the 'hand-lead... constantly going' even in pilot-waters. Updated in 1806 these regulations stated that a pilot intended for temporary service had to be 'borne on a list of supernumeraries for Wages and Victuals, and shall

---

27 James, *ibid*, 94.
28 Bigland, *ibid*, 484.
29 Irving, 1813, 468.
30 Massey, *ibid*, 350.
31 1787, pages 222/223.

be discharged as soon as the service is performed'.[32] While embarked he received an enclosed berth, hammock and bedding and was considered on par with 'warrant Officers'.[33] He was paid local rates for the ports he worked. For Thames and Nore waters only pilots licensed by Trinity House of Deptford Strond could be employed.

After the Battle of Copenhagen the British fleet departed in fine fettle but their passage 'through the narrow channel, between the Island of Amag and that of Saltholm, called the Grounds, was attended with some difficulty'.[34] Two or three heavy ships ran aground and were refloated only after they had removed their guns. As they did so Prussian and Dutch troops had marched by land to seize British estates in and around Hanover to shut them off from British influence, trade and commerce. Unaware of this development the British fleet sailed into the Baltic. Off Bornholm island they touched upon a Swedish squadron which turned and made for Karlskrona. They were given chase upon a deep blue sea until they approached the green fringe of islands in front of the port. The *Dart* (28) was sent in with offers of a truce that when received by Gustav IV Adolf, Sweden's king, was readily agreed to although that monarch stubbornly maintained adherence to the 'Northern Confederacy'. However, three days later a lugger arrived with shocking and quite unexpected news: Russia's mad Tsar Paul had been murdered; and the new tsar, Alexander, was all for peace. Admiral Parker therefore loitered near Denmark, was soon relieved by the admiralty and Nelson given command. Never one for inaction the vice admiral immediately set sail for Revel. But it was too late. Ice had long since thawed and the Russian fleet was united at Cronstadt. Communications were opened and although it took time for all parties to reach an agreement a convention was signed with Russia on 17 June 1801. Sequestered British estates in Germany were returned. This Baltic campaign came to an end.

The Danish pilot was a long term immigrant to Britain. There were many like him. Europe had suffered nine years of war with consequent rupture, division and forced movement of families. France had particularly suffered due to her revolution. Hippolyte Taine later wrote, 'It was found convenient to manufacture an émigré in order to confiscate his possessions.'[35] Some 200,000 French émigrés were therefore displaced,

---

32 1806, 199.

33 *Regulations and Instructions Relating to His Majesty's Service at Sea,* ibid, 200.

34 Robinson G. and J., *ibid,* 'COP'. Amag, or Amager.

35 Taine, 1885, 292.

either within France or abroad, to Coblentz,[36] Hamburg[37], London, and other cities. It was the same for Dutch and German peoples. Some willingly emigrated. One gentleman, with interests in the carrying trade, elected to leave Lübeck and settle in Plymouth. British bottoms could no longer deal with demand, so ships with foreign crews had been permitted to carry British trade. He was part of a steady trickle of Germans who left their homeland, mostly Hessians and southern peasants who migrated to America; that flow was soon to become a deluge. Oliver Oldschool wrote in 1802, 'It is remarkable that even the lowest class of northern Germans are never, or at most very seldom pleased with America. Perhaps the principal cause of this may be, because there are so many southern Germans there.'[38] The German gentleman was disdainful of southern Catholics. The German trader's move resulted in the purchase of a large property with fine views of Dartmoor. He soon found that as a foreigner he was not alone. Plymouth and Dock were crowded with sailors from far off lands. Manpower had been short from the start of the war so Parliament had decreed in 1794 'An Act for the further Encouragement of British Mariners; and for other Purposes therein Mentioned'.[39] This allowed foreign sailors to work British fishing vessels 'not exceeding One-fourth of the Number of Mariners on board.'[40] Thus it was expedient to have foreigners sailors declared to be British, and 'every Foreign Sailor' who served in the war for three years would receive a certificate 'testifying his faithful Service and Good Behaviour'. Those who then made an oath of allegiance to His Majesty would in peace time be entitled to employment on a warship or be declared a British sailor. He could make his oath in either London, Chatham, Portsmouth or Plymouth, at a small cost of course. So the German gentleman heard German, Danish, Spanish, Portuguese, French, Indian and Russian accents almost everywhere he went.

The gentleman developed the habit of making regular visits to Sutton Pool in Plymouth for he loved to observe the merchant vessels that lay there and hear their news from abroad. When his own vessels lay amongst them his heart swelled with pride.

While on passage to the Baltic and Elbe river his ships' safety was his first obsession. Once he had lost a vessel of sixty tons burthen to a privateer.

---

36 Zimmermann, 1878, 1630.

37 Stephens, 1891, 506.

38 Oldschool, 1802, 353.

39 *The Statutes at Large*, 1794, 558.

40 *Ibid*, 558.

But he was heartened by the protective shield British warships provided. He knew he would not be able to conduct his trade without them.

For many residents of British sea towns, the fortunes of the Royal Navy were a dominant interest. Some acquaintances the German made thought him more patriotic than any natural born 'Englisher'. He would raise a glass of Hock, thank the navy, liken Britain to the fabled maelstrom – in this case a vortex of commerce – and bark out, 'Trade in *und* trade out!'

His newfound 'patriotism' reached fever pitch at the start of the new century. A wave of excitement swept through Dock, the yard, the hospital, Citadel, Plymouth and even Mill Prison. Nelson received the freedom of the city and the German got to see his hero in the flesh! On 24 January 1801 the city corporation presented the newly promoted vice admiral with a silver box. The weather was terribly cold with sleet and snow so he struggled to hear the mayor's speech. Only later, in the comfort of his home, did he read the address. What he did not read was Nelson's private correspondence dated two days later in which the vice admiral wrote, 'I hate Plymouth'.[41]

Lübeck was always on the gentleman's mind – he sorely missed the green spires and bells of the Marienkirche and the taste of fresh herring – but his new home offered many compensations. Plymouth and Dock were hives of activity. The German's belly broadcast the fact he liked his food and Dock market operated three days a week. He quickly discovered a spot on high wasteland outside Plymouth called the Hoe, between the stone-clad Citadel and Red Beacon, where he would stand and gaze upon the sound so often choked with fishing boats and vessels of all kinds. Pilchards and John Dory were hauled onto the quays most days and he procured much for both his ships and his personal larder.

Because of the war, other produce was not always cheap. Pork was now sadly rare, with large amounts swept up by the navy, and after two bad seasons beef and mutton prices had risen.[42] Supplies of corn were precarious. In 1803 Robert Bissett wrote how Parliament discussed national scarcity: 'Acts were passed for enjoining, for a specified time, the use of mixed and inferior kinds of bread... . Recommendations were added to all families and individuals, to be as economical as possible in the use of bread. Distillation of spirits was also suspended, that luxury might not employ grain, so much wasted for necessaries.'[43]

For the British nation nine years of war had caused many hardships but 1801 became 'distinguished by the exorbitant price of necessaries

---

41 Pettigrew, 1849, 417; and Hamilton, 1894, 109.

42 Tooke, 1823, 74.

43 Bissett, 1803, 722.

of life'.[44] Bread riots broke out in Birmingham in May and September.[45] The quality of an average loaf deteriorated, noticeable even for a new arrival like the German. But he cared little for that for he much preferred a hunk of honest dark rye bread. He was delighted when he found a local woman who would bake it for him and he tasked his captains to ensure they arrived in Plymouth with rye flour, as well as a whole range of German produce. People struggled to put food on the table, but he noted with satisfaction that Plymouth's extensive victualling offices continued to supply the 'national service'.[46]

Apart from food for the body the German was also interested in food for the soul. He gleefully patronised circulating libraries in Dock and Plymouth. Von Schlegel's words, 'The historian is a prophet looking backwards,'[47] always pleased him. He reckoned himself to be an historian, but no Jeremiah for he perceived only the good in events; especially events to do with his new-found darlings, the seamen of the Royal Navy.

He studied the Battle of Copenhagen and collected as many books as he could on the subject. He purchased a copy of a survey made by a Swedish admiral, Nordenanker, of which it was said, 'There can be no doubt that the shores, shoals, &c. &c. are laid down with the utmost accuracy'.[48] Together with other charts he found or paid for – of Zealand, the Little and Great Belt and the Sound ('the key of the Baltic'[49]) – they spent the whole summer of 1801 on his bedside table. He would consult them whenever he reread Nelson's account of *Edgar*'s 'intrepidity', damage to the *Isis*, how bomb-ships had thrown 'some shells in to the arsenal' and how captured Danish ships had been made 'sieves'. He concluded it must have been a most splendid action, one he would have liked to have seen, at a safe distance.

A copy of the *Naval Chronicle*, a new publication he considered a wonderful innovation, provided him with a useful table of Danish losses: *Holsteen*, *Jylland*, *Suerfisken*, *Kronborg* all taken; *Charlotte Amalie*, *Indfodstratten*, *Provesteen*, *Sohesten* and *Vagrien* taken and burnt; *Rendsborg* driven onto shoals; *Dannebrog* burned.[50] It made him think the battle so very exciting, far better than anything he had ever read in a novel!

44 Watts, 1806, 185.
45 Dickens, 1869, 464.
46 Watts, *ibid*, 186.
47 Found in von Schlegel's *Athenaeum Volume I*, as mentioned in Bent, 1887, 87; first published in the 1790s.
48 Smollett, 1802, page 586.
49 Charnock, 1806, 212
50 *Volume VI*, 1801, 120.

So informed, he liked to barrage his guests with his opinion that Denmark had thought herself safe behind her fortresses and Sound *until British naval supremacy had destroyed that notion.* Any suggestions that Nelson had become annoyed with Admiral Parker's leadership, that he had deliberately ignored his signal, were swept aside. He considered Vice Admiral Nelson's conduct irreproachable!

Throughout the summer of 1801 the activities of Lord Nelson remained the centre of interest for those who lived along England's south coast.[51] Disappointed with the dissolution of the northern league Napoléon had re-raised the spectre of invasion. After the vice admiral returned to Britain a clamour was made to have him take command of a flying squadron to deal with it. 'Boulogne was the point from which it was supposed the invasion might be attempted.'[52] Nelson embarked on a new ship at the Downs and was off there by 2 August 1801. Two days later his bomb ships sunk a few floating batteries and disturbed two brigs, but he wrote, 'I own that this boat warfare is not exactly congenial to my feelings; and I find that I get laughed at for my puny mode of attack.... [but] whilst I serve, I shall do it actively, and to the very best of my abilities.'[53] He found the French flotilla and invasion flat boats to be well moored and protected from the shore. He failed to burn, destroy or cause the French to sail out and lost 172 men killed and wounded in doing so.

In consequence the German gentleman concluded, in line with Nelson's public statements, that with a night attack and a difficult coast nothing more could have been done. Any other commander might have been condemned but a hero never could. Anyway, the next month British forces captured Alexandria. The Royal Navy remained in the ascendant! The gentleman joined a crowd at the assembly rooms to sing the obligatory refrain on all such occasions:

Rule Britannia!,
Britannia rules the waves,
Britons never will be slaves!

However, this war had dragged on for far too long. More than eight years of effort, blood, and material had been expended. People prayed for peace. Preliminaries for such were made on 1 October 1801, and when peace was

---

51 Collins, 1812, 608.
52 Massey, *ibid,* 360.
53 Collins, *ibid,* 608.

certain, delirious joy broke out. It seemed all 19,000 Plymouth residents took to the streets. Church bells pealed and mobs of drunks regaled all and sundry. The German held a splendid dinner and at its conclusion stood up, none too steadily, to make a toast: *Ladies und gentlemen, der King! To increased commerce wit United America!*

Peace allowed an evaluation of the war and conduct of the fleets by the new first lord of the admiralty, Lord St Vincent. A visit to a naval yard had found 'persons… [who had] contrived to get appointed as Warrant Officers on board some of his Majesty's ships, who had not been brought up in the navy'.[54] The admiralty had responded to this with regulations upon length of service required before promotion to certain positions. It was, for example, stipulated: 'No person to be appointed a Purser, who has not served two years as Secretary or Clerk to a Flag Officer, or Captain's Clerk of his Majesty's ships' etc. There was clearly a need to look into cases of abuse, fraud and embezzlement if the senior service was to serve the British Empire and help her win a future war. It was time to put away the spyglass, eager to find an enemy sail on the horizon, and take up the pen to root out corruption ashore.

---

54 *The European Magazine Vol 42*, 1802, 478.

Chapter 2

And Guardian Angels Sang this Strain

Come in, get out of the cold. Belay those noddies[55] fighting. Take a seat. I'm the bluffer[56] of this place.

You look a couple of trim lads. I heard you humming 'The Saucy Arethusa.'[57] Tars, are ye? Got some leave, or did you jump ship? Ahh, paid off! More of your sorts ashore now the war's over. Got some coin then? Wages and prize money I'll bet.

So, what do you want? Grog or ale? Care for company? Nice girls, none of your dowdies trolling[58] the streets with ragged and worn vampers.[59] All clean and none of 'em from a nanny house. No buttock and files here.

Where were you two dragged up? I ain't heard your crazy jabber[60] afore. Orkney!? Where's that away, Scotland? Well, I never.

Hungry? Want some belly timber?[61] Beth! See if we've any more of that mutton pasty.

What did they call you on your ship? Gog and Magog? 'Steep tub' and 'Barrel'? Ha! - you've got some of the broadest shoulders I've ever seen. I bet you can handle yourselves, eh?

Lean in lads and listen. Enjoy your pay but I guess you're a long way from home. Unless you get passage you'll soon be at a loose end. Nowhere to stay? I could introduce you to someone who'd offer you a means to earn payment. You could afford lodgings then. Understand?

---

55 Fools. Found in: *A New Canting Dictionary: Comprehending all the Terms, Ancient and Modern, used in the several tribes etc,* 1725. All slang used from this source. 'Belay' was and still is a nautical term for 'ignore'.

56 Host.

57 A popular tune at the time.

58 Loitering. A *doudy* was an ugly woman.

59 Stockings. A 'nanny house' was a brothel; a 'buttock and file' a 'whore and pickpocket.'

60 Fast talk.

61 Food.

Good. See that man with an F on his cheek? That's Turley, our dimber-damber.[62] *Dimber… ain't you never heard of the word? He's second only to our Upright Man.*[63] *He'd give you work and not in vain. As they say, 'Let Him Labour That Wants.'*

What sort of work? Well, seeing as you're tars an all he'd probably give you a baggage of scrawny woman and babe and send you inland to tour and regale audiences with tales of battle and life at sea. He'd get a crowd up all eager like and you'd tell 'em how you saved the girl and child from certain shipwreck and a French prison. People love to hear such things and they pay for it too. You'd go snacks,[64] *see? Take care though, no one would understand a word you two would say so perhaps not. Ah well, I guess a few whipjacks*[65] *will have to do.*

If not that, then our tumblers[66] *could do with a hand. My cousin would hire you two quicker than a fiddler's elbow. You'd have no trouble knowing who he is for he's a mannikin*[67] *no taller than four feet. He may be a pickeroon but he delivers wood to the yard, see. Not that God awful foreign stuff that lands yonder at the Master Attendant's Stairs. Nor that warty lot from up river. No, true solid oak from inland. Only the best from my cuz. He has a pass, see, and he rattles in and out the gate no problem. He's no dandy prat*[68] *either. The porters never stop him.*

Well, he drops his loads down at the pond - you know, where they float masts to keep 'em from cracking? - and then he brings out wood chips from the timber yard all bundled up for auction. Well, there are some tartars[69] *who'd rob his tumbler before he could ever tip us a few items. You'd be his guards to make them think twice, see?*

Not sure?

Well then, we could get you labouring in the yard. They always need men. You'd be hard put to it, shifting heavy stuff all day, but on occasion they still allow you to carry out wood-chips for personal use and yous two could

---

62 Brewer, 1895, 436. The 'prince' of a crew or second in charge. The branded F meant he had been found guilty of brawling in a churchyard. The custom was not abolished by law until 1822.

63 An 'Upright Man' was canting dialect for a chief or leader of a gang.

64 Share.

65 Men who pretended to be a sailors.

66 Carts.

67 A dwarf.

68 Insignificant fellow.

69 A rogue's rogue who would rob other robbers. A 'prigg' was similar.

shift a load on both shoulders no doubt about it! That'd be a rare sight to see: you two puffing and wheezing as you staggered through the gate!

And if you don't ask questions, didn't mind them bundles being a bit heavier than usual now and then, and didn't take a peek inside... well, we pay the porters to gather wool.[70] Get my meaning? And if by an off chance you were hampered you would only have to act leaden. With your accents they'd lose interest soon enough. Attend mind, we look after our own. There's always a dozen affidavit men[71] for hire. Something you could do now and then.

What do you say? Will you bell-the-cat[72] and earn a pretty penny? Help out those sadly adrift? There's always a henpecked or conveniency[73] that looks forward to a windfall. Blocks and rope make a small fortune. You'd never be sent anywhere near the gunwharf, barracks or Governor's House. Nothing you wouldn't mind doing, I'm sure. Besides, we keep the beadles in line.

You will? Good! Then yam[74] and I'll take you over to meet Turley. The next bowse is on me. Good timing too. There's lately been a few rum looking bollocks down from the Admiralty, all questions and no by your leave. As you otters say,[75] a squall is coming. Best to make hay while the sun still shines, eh?

On 1 October 1801, 9 Vendémiaire X to the French, a preliminary treaty of fifteen articles was made between His Majesty the King of the United Kingdom of Great Britain and Ireland and the First Consul of the French Republic. It aimed to restore amity between the two powers both by land and sea 'in all parts of the world'. The first article set out to return to France, the Batavian Republic and Spain all captured colonies acquired by Britain during the war 'with the exception of the Island of Trinidad, and the Dutch possessions in the island of Ceylon'.[76] Malta was ostensibly restored to the Knights of St John of Jerusalem, Egypt to the Sublime Porte, and Naples and Rome evacuated of all French occupation. Further articles stated that released prisoners would be allowed to return home without ransom; all captured forts would be relinquished; Newfoundland fisheries restored to

---

70 To make a serious but useless inquiry.
71 False witnesses.
72 Commit to the danger of a shared enterprise.
73 Husband and wife.
74 Eat lustily.
75 Sailor.
76 Steel, 1806, 112.

how they had been before the war. Inhabitants of restored colonies were to be left alone to live a life free from molestation; and because of delays with news reaching far abroad prizes taken *after* the date of the treaty would be returned.

Twenty-two articles were formalised at Amiens on 27 March 1802 between the British, French, Spanish and Dutch contingencies, signed by Marquis Cornwallis, Citizen Joseph Bonaparte and the plenipotentiaries J. Nicolas de Azara and R. J. Schimmelpenninck. The Peace was proclaimed in London on 29 April 1802.

The British had given up many territories gained by conquest, but these would have been expensive to maintain. Alfred Thayer Mahan, a US naval officer, later reckoned those Britain did retain 'were important as depots of trade, as well as for strategic reasons'.[77]

What was not complained about was how the tally of captured warships proved highly favourable to the Royal Navy. *Steel's Naval Chronologist* reckoned the British then had 361 French, 98 Dutch, 93 Spanish and 16 Danish-built ships from a total of 570 captures; opposed to 59 ships lost by the British. Eighty-six of those foreign captures were valuable line ships[78] (though William James stated this number to be fifty because he did not include ineffective ships in his calculations[79]).

An anonymous author called 'Britannicus' wrote to the *Naval Chronicle* in 1801[80] of how the navy stood that year as compared to 1791, 'shewing the amazing addition... received... at the expense of our enemies'. A further, more detailed, abstract laid out the full naval force in commission at the start of 1802: 4 first rates, 15 second rates and 85 third rates for a total of 104 line ships; 11 fourth rates, 111 fifth rates, 24 sixth rates and 92 sloops.[81] It must be said though that William James disagreed with *Steel's* list and others. He even argued how 'typographical error' had been a cause of confusion. Few accounts tally with each other.

There were also those who worked the ships. During the first five months of 1802 this amounted to more than 130,000 men and women,[82] which dropped down to 70,000 towards the end of the year. Both men and ships had to be paid for. It was reported to Parliament's Committee of Ways and

---

77 Mahan, 1902, 73.
78 Steel, *ibid,* 102.
79 James, Vol III, 239.
80 *Vol VI,* 1801, 281.
81 *Abstracts of the British Navy* etc.
82 James, *ibid,* 237.

Means that for the first five months of 1802, 'The estimates of the Navy already voted' stood at £7,770,896.[83] But with peace it was obvious so many ships and their complements were no longer needed.

Naval seamen faced an uncertain future. Some worried that if released en masse, would they receive their arrears of wages in full? Could so many find employment elsewhere? The merchant service was a possibility, as was industry, but neither were certain. At least officers above the rank of lieutenant received half pay when not in service or retired, given out quarterly.

To release so many people back into civil society ran the perceived risk of causing 'mischief', especially if those released did not receive their dues. The *Naval Chronicle* ran an article which stated, 'Robberies and murders, it is well known, have too often been the unhappy effects attending a reduction of our Navy.'[84] Furthermore, those sailors unwilling to work or seek lawful employment could fall prey to nefarious gangs and canting crews. Many around Britain and Ireland seethed with rebellion and insurrection. The topic of discharge of sailors was considered by another anonymous writer, 'Neptune', in an article that opened with the words 'Britons never will be slaves.'[85] He wondered, 'when we turn our thoughts to the immense number and extraordinary character of those seamen who we are to expect will in a short time be set at liberty, and when we reflect, that although we have no longer a foreign, we have innumerable domestic enemies, more dangerous than the former, some system must be adopted in order to keep those brave fellows from contamination at home, who have by their unexampled courage obtained immortal honour abroad.' He proposed full payment of wages and prize money for married men and those who had previously had employment. The remainder ought, he argued, be retained for guardship and foreign duty. As to senior naval officers a strong corps ought to be maintained to ensure their experience and naval knowledge would be carried on into the next era.

As it turned out, the peace was little more than an armed truce.[86] Sloops and vessels were sold off 'but few, if any, Frigates or large Ships'.[87] For those released, arrears of wages were doled out either by clerks of the cheque in naval dockyards, at customs houses, or at the Navy Pay Office

---

83 Urban, 1802, 667.
84 *Naval Chronicle*, ibid, 285.
85 *Naval Chronicle*, ibid, 283.
86 Mahan, *ibid*, 77.
87 Derrick, 1806, 217.

in London. It was assumed that Irish, Welsh and Scottish sailors would be 'conveyed' homewards by ship. The risk of fraud was all too obvious and captains were encouraged to make proper lists of all sailors released from their complements.

Fraud and embezzlement within the service, by those who would make the war effort one of low traffic, was of interest to many. A woman who retired in 1801 from nursing at the Royal Hospital East Stonehouse and on the *Caton* – an old 64-gun warship converted to a hospital ship – afterwards liked to sit in her small garden and gaze out over Sutton Pool, the Cattewater and the Hoe. She received countless callers during her retirement, mostly old acquaintances and work colleagues who came to pass on news of their families, national events and new fashions. She would share a cup of tea, eat some wondrous cakes, and be intensely aware that the old ways were passing. Abolitionists, evangelicals and a series of government enquiries had brought about great changes and she came to believe that a new sensibility arose at the time of Amiens. In 1803 the nurse heard how an offhand remark made by Mr Robson, 'member for Okehampton', upon a trifling bill of £19.13.0 presented to the Sick and Hurt Office not honoured due lack of public monies, had occasioned him to wonder whether the government was insolvent.[88] *Insolvent!?* she told her niece, *How awful if true!* She had worried about that – for the Royal Navy was their wooden wall – and she had been gratified to hear that Viscount Sidmouth would look into the matter. At the suggestion of Earl St Vincent – *such a great but stern man!* – 'the whole of the Naval Department was fixed upon'.[89] *Nothing new*, a visitor had said, *for numerous government reports had been made about naval administration in the past*. He told her how clerks of the admiralty first received salaries in 1796 to end peculation.

In her time the nurse had heard countless rumours and conjecture about naval corruption. Such as how impress officers often took bribes not to press a merchant ship's crew[90]; that agents could be dishonest or deliberately wasteful; that fleets had to shoulder a 'long precarious and unsafe dependence upon the Contractors and Merchant-builders' as the Victualling Office had 'officers appointed by interest alone, and a system of barefaced peculation... carried on by those who had the duty of provisioning the fleet, for the ships were furnished in a great degree by contract through

---

88 Phillips, *Public Characters of 1806* printed the same year.
89 Phillips, *ibid*, 583.
90 Trotter, 1819, 18.

the purser.'[91] Therefore, thanks to the member for Okehampton, it did not surprise her when an act was made on 29 December 1802 titled *'For appointing Commissioners to inquire and examine into any Irregularities, Frauds or Abuses, which are or have been practised by Persons employed in the several Naval Departments therein mentioned, and in the Business of Prize Agency, and to report such Observations as shall occur to them for preventing such Irregularities, Frauds, and Abuses, and for the better conducting and managing the Business of the said Departments, and of Prize Agency, in future.'*[92]

The naval departments inspected ranged from the very top down to the management of yards, prisons and hospital ships. Five nominated commissioners, under auspices of the Commons,[93] made their oaths and received authority to employ their own clerks and officers and call upon any related person, document, record or contract for their inspection. They were given powers to imprison anyone who refused to be inspected, or hindered their inquiry, until such persons cooperated. But so far as she knew no one was ever compelled to submit a document or make a statement that might have incriminated themselves. Eventually the five commissioners, Vice Admiral Charles Pole, Hugh Leycester, Ewan Law, John Ford and Henry Nichols, revealed a level of corruption and neglect the nurse likened to the Augean stables.[94] Some of their findings became of interest to the nation.

The nurse's brother had been a naval officer – *God bless his memory!* – and with the aid of his old spyglass she kept watch on the hundreds of ships which made their slow way in and out of the Sound. She cared little for their types and class, only that they gave her comfort. Ships similar to *Caton* she understood a little better, but never their sail plans nor rigging. *Such splendid sights with their tall masts and broad sails. Now, what were the names of the ships my brother served on?*

The commissioners' 'First Report' was presented to the House of Commons on 12 May 1803 and later printed in Volume Nine of the *Naval Chronicle*.[95] On a windy day the nurse had a copy of that periodical read to her by the marine son of a dear friend. *Such a handsome man in his uniform. What is his name?* The pages of the *Chronicle* flapped about him as he told

---

91 Bright, 1837, 1194.

92 Pickering, 1804, 19.

93 Not under the Lords, nor under Royal sanction.

94 The Fifth Labour of Hercules was to clean a stables; the phrase was common in the era and referred to the cleaning away of corruption.

95 1803, page 441 onwards.

her of 'the conduct of Naval Storekeepers abroad… it being apprehended that considerable abuses had been practiced'[96] with bills of exchange.

'Supposedly,' the marine said, 'Mr William Smith, naval storekeeper at Jamaica, had been dismissed in 1796 for 'not giving Government credit for the premium of his bills.'[97]

The nurse had no idea what that meant. 'What had he done?'

'Gross fraud, ma'am.'

'How so?'

'Well, ma'am, a mast that might have been purchased from England – Dock perhaps – at a cost of £198.18.8 was instead purchased from America for £1,238.0.0!'[98]

'Oh? A simple mistake then?'

'No, ma'am, for cables and ropes from England that would have cost £4,421.19.5 were charged by Mr Smith at £13,307.10.0.'[99]

'I see. Is that usual?'

'No, ma'am. The commissioners wonder how it so long escaped the observation of the Navy Board.'

The nurse smiled knowingly at that remark for she knew all about the Navy Board. 'Was he punished?'

'Not by the navy, ma'am, for he is in the Fleet Prison for debt.'

'Oh, poor dear to be brought so low.'

Further reports were published and the nurse read them or had them read to her. The second one looked into the Chest at Chatham, a fund for maimed and wounded seamen, that showed evidence of fraud. *For shame, how could they!?* The commissioners thought it improper that a sailor maimed and made limbless in service of his country should have to make his way to Chatham to receive his 'benefit'. So the chest was removed to Greenwich Hospital. *Those brave men, to be treated so cruel.* A third report focused on 'Block and Cooper's Contracts' and revealed 'mistakes' made with contracts. A fourth report considered prize agency and showed 'abuses and irregularities, rather than fraud' (a recommendation for a General Prize Office was made nonetheless). *They are abuses, however!* A fifth report considered irregularities with the 'Sixpenny Office', a means to collect sailors' contributions of sixpence per month to fund Greenwich Hospital, that found two of the three men supposed to manage the fund lived nowhere

---

96 *Naval Chronicle,* ibid, 441. The terms of abuses that follow are from this source.

97 *Naval Chronicle,* ibid, 441.

98 Phillips, *ibid,* 585.

99 *Ibid.*

near the hospital. All these reports were not worthy of much interest to the nurse. The ones that followed were.

The sixth report considered the Woolwich and Plymouth dockyards. Charles Derrick, employed by the Navy Office, penned in 1806 how 'three months after the signing of the preliminaries of peace' there had been in all British naval yards £2,610,908 of 'unappropriated stores' of which Plymouth held more than anywhere else with £611,819.[100] Stores included anchors, blocks, boards, cables, canvas, copper sheets, hemp, iron, masts, pitch, spars, tar, timber, treenails, turpentine and yards. Such quantities had been open to plunder despite an act of 1698 that punished illicit possession of anything with a broad arrow,[101] the sign stamped on naval stores and materials.

The nurse intimately knew Dock's naval yard for she had visited on many occasions to attend the injured. It had been built on the east side of the Hamoaze, that part of the river Tamar some four miles in length and about half a mile wide where ships could be moored to swing with the tide and prison hulks lay.[102] *Yes,* she told her daughter's sluggard of a Dorsetshire husband, *it is a vibrant and busy place. Have you ever visited? No, I suppose not. Well, let me tell you about it.* And she proceeded to tell him how it dominated the town. Workers therein laboured three-for-one shifts (*three normal days' effort in one day, sir!*) and she knew many of the men and their families. *They work so hard, something that should inspire all of us.* In some places the enclosing wall, which stretched from North Corner to Mutton Cove along Queen Street, reached thirty feet in height and three porters and two marines guarded the foot passenger and main gate with two 6-pounders at the ready.[103] Officers came and went by a smaller wicket gate. *It is always well protected, sir.*

Just inside the yard's main gate a time bell had been erected and some of the buildings were less than forty years old, for *the yard is relatively new.* There was a chapel and pay office and houses for the master porter, master shipwright, master's attendant, clerk of the cheque, clerk of the survey, clerk of the rope-yard, storekeeper, surgeon and boatswain. To the north were the stairs – *where my brother always landed* – and access to a pitch house, a double dock, single dock[104] and a joiner's shop. *I have seen the basin and*

---

100 Derrick, *ibid*, 216.
101 The act was 9 and 10 Will. III c. 41.
102 Gilbert, 1817, 399.
103 *The Tourist Companion*, 1823, 158.
104 The largest then in Great Britain.

let me tell you, sir, it is of massive proportions. Ships larger than Caton *can be put in there* – but she did not mention how she had never dared stand too close to the edge in case she fell in. She told of the south yard with its rigging house '480 feet long, and three stories high, forming one side of a quadrangle'[105] together with a sail loft and other store houses; how a slip allowed ships and vessels to be hauled up and graved[106] with a boat house for repairs; that a long canal formed a barrier beyond which was the 'new ground' with its blacksmith's shop of constant clamour and moving cranes and an anchor wharf and slips where large anchors and warships were built close beside a boiling-house for steaming masts. A mast house produced masts that for first rates stood more than a hundred feet tall and ten feet wide; they were floated in a large pond until requisitioned. She had the sluggard husband fetch her a book and open it to where it said, 'The [wood] chips which arise from converting timber to the requisite shapes, were formerly carried out of the Yard, as a perquisite by the workmen, in bundles; to form which, not only a large quantity of good timber was frequently destroyed, but articles of more value secreted in them. This occasioned an order that no more should be taken from the yard; and Government allows each man sixpence a day in lieu of them. The chips are now sold by auction once every fortnight.'[107] *You should see those auctions, sir!* The rope house made large and dangerous looking cables. *Some are twenty-five inches in circumference, like so, and more than 100 fathoms long. Quite monstrous to behold.* But she wondered whether the sluggard had a mind to imagine such things. There was a mould loft, and overlooking everything a watch house and powder house on Bunker's Hill. *The yard is a dangerous place where men labour amid great heat and noise. I have seen terrible injuries there.*

Three further reports, the seventh to the ninth, looked into the situation at Plymouth. These were of great interest to the nurse and her close circle for they considered the *Caton* hospital ship, the naval hospital, the Victualling Office, and the yard. Irregularities, neglect and gross frauds were found with embezzlement of victualling casks and issuing of stores. The purser on the hospital ship, Samuel Keast, was said to have maintained 'a very extravagant table'[108] defrayed out of the 'profits of his contract' in collusion with the surgeon. She couldn't say whether this was true or not, for she had long left the service by then, but she had heard rumours. There was always

---

105 *The Picture of Plymouth,* 1812, 105.
106 Cleaned.
107 *The Picture of Plymouth,* ibid, 177.
108 *The Parliamentary Debates,* 1805, 1098.

tittle-tattle to hear and most reached her ear. And the men who managed affairs in the yard seemed to have neglected their duties.

Thomas Netherton, First Clerk to the Clerk of the Check of His Majesty's Yard at Plymouth brought together men required to work the yard and he maintained accounts of expenses. He underwent examination in 1803[109] and his testimony brought to light numerous small derelictions. He said that he did not have clear guidelines as to his role, nor did he understand regulations for his expected conduct. He could not state specific instructions that had been issued by the Navy Board. An implication he made was that wages of artificers and labourers – the builders, foremen, joiners, oakum boys, shipwrights and pitch-heaters – had not altered since 1784 which had caused situations where the men had often 'struck work'.[110]

The nurse knew how people struggled to pay for bread and daily necessaries. Who didn't? Did poor pay encourage theft? She assumed it must have done. It was said that shipwrights in Plymouth earned far less than those in Portsmouth.[111] Smuggling occurred all along the coast, had done so for years, despite hundreds of naval ships on the lookout. Cawsand,[112] directly south of the sound, and the Yealm river to the east, had long been favourite anchorages for vessels involved in that illicit trade. She remembered how, in 1799, a lugger under Lieutenant Elliott had captured a smuggling cutter with 300 ankers of spirits and tobacco onboard. Pilfered items could easily be brought in and out of the many coves and bays. She knew a woman who sold claret at a 'favourable' price and had purchased two bottles to help celebrate her daughter's fiftieth birthday. *Goes so well with this plum cake*[113] *don't you think, dear?*

It was the tenth report, dated 13 February 1805, that gained the most public interest as it lead to the impeachment of Viscount Melville. The old nurse heatedly discussed everything about this over a delicious seed cake with two male guests and a woman who would not stop talking. The men explained how monies for the navy were placed in the Bank of England and withdrawn by the Naval Treasurer when required. But Viscount Melville (Henry Dundas) 'drew large sums out of the Bank, and placed the same in the hands of Messrs. Coutts and Co., bankers in the Strand, giving drafts in

---

109 *Naval Chronicle Vol XV,* 1806, 212 to 215.
110 A possible origin of the phrase 'to strike', when people refuse to work, comes from the navy – to 'strike' was to lower a ship's sails.
111 *Cobbett's Parliamentary Debates*, 1805, 1013.
112 *Naval Chronicle Vol II*, 1799, 543.
113 Briggs, 1788, 527.

payment upon them, not only to answer the demands of the Treasurer of the Navy, but likewise on Mr. Dundas's private account.'[114] When interviewed, Melville's agent had refused to answer questions upon sums withdrawn, estimated to be £6,000,000; and when asked to provide accounts between 1785 and 1800, Melville answered he was unable to do so as he had already left office. The enquiry eventually concluded that Melville used 'to a great amount' monies for 'private emolument'. The talkative lady's face turned red with anger when she heard about *such impropriety*.

By then the large number of reports had dredged up so much mud that the increasingly frail nurse fretted over what they meant for her beloved navy. And they continued to be published for years thereafter. Corruption within the Victualling Board was reported to Parliament on 12 March 1809[115] with the 'Tenth Report of The Commissioners of Naval Revision'. It talked of a 'disastrous state of the Imprests' (amounts of monies) within the Board and the nature of improper appointments. Arrears of accounts with the Victualling Board were thought to be 'most loud', and abuses and fraud had been reported ever since 1786. In 1806 the amount of monies unsettled by this Board stood at £10,985,100. It was suggested to have men in office of 'real ability, professional knowledge, and uninterrupted industry' if the navy was to end such neglect. An eleventh report considered bills used to raise monies and how the Navy Board had issued some for 'secret naval services'.[116] £95,000 was not accounted for, although it was argued this sum could not be divulged as services paid for had 'still not terminated'.

The nurse hoped something would be done because these enquiries put the Royal Navy in such a bad light. An old friend argued that *the sick patient had to be purged of disease!* Yes, the nurse thought, unless the remedy was more dangerous.

Later, in 1815, the nurse did not agree with an *Enquiry into the present state of the British Navy etc by an Englishman*. It argued how 450 of 840 naval captains achieved their rank on merit, while the remainder gained theirs 'purely by private patronage, and borough interest' and a 'fortunate possession of friends'[117]. *What of it?* she complained. Patronage and preferment helped her brother gain his step on the seniority list, and he had served with distinction. The book annoyed her. *Everyone nowadays wants to question and quibble about how things are done.*

---

114 Phillips, *ibid*, 588.
115 Hansard, 1812, 746 to 749.
116 *Cobbett's Parliamentary Debates,* 1812, x.
117 p.45.

The nurse and her guests conversed more upon news of battles, heroes and other events than they did about investigations. For instance, how during the peace France had gained Spanish possessions in North America, had tried to gain Portuguese lands in Brazil, that she had intervened in Switzerland, how Napoléon had ascended to First Consul for life and then Emperor, the Battle of Trafalgar, and the War of 1812. One particularly happy time was when Evan Nepean signed a statement (dated 29 April 1802) that read, *'His Majesty had been graciously pleased to signify His Commands, that, in consideration of the very meritorious services of the Marines during the late War, the Corps shall in future be styled "The Royal Marines." By Command of their Lordships'*. It did not take long for the marine to call and show off his new jacket with blue facings[118] similar, he said, to the Royal infantry.

After Bonaparte sailed off to final exile the nurse declined. Memories of conversations jumbled in her mind and she started to talk to people not there. In February 1816 she retired to her sick bed. One cold afternoon her dead brother appeared at the foot of her bed. She held out a frail hand and called his name. Her family, sitting around the room, looked up and the doctor told them she was delirious. By the time her hand fell back to her side she had passed away. Her daughter gently closed the curtains.

---

118 Cannon, 1850, 47.

Chapter 3

The Dread and Envy of them All

On a very cold winter's day in early 1806, a party of junior petty officers met three sisters of one of their old shipmates. The three women had travelled far and everyone wore their best.

BLUE BONNET. Nelson has gone to Heaven then, like so many others.

WELSHMAN. To be sure. A first rate could not stop them.[119]

WHITE GLOVES. What happened to your right ear?

ENGLISHMAN. A splinter took it off courtesy of a Spanish ball. Doesn't look pretty, does it?

YELLOW SHAWL. Did it hurt?

ENGLISHMAN. Terribly. Can't hear a thing with it now. The other is almost as useless.

WHITE GLOVES. Poor man.

WELSHMAN. You can't imagine the noise of guns 'tween decks. They knock you senseless after a while. No wonder he went half-deaf.

YELLOW SHAWL. Once, as a little girl, I heard a great gun go off and I didn't stop running until my father caught me.

WHITE GLOVES. Could you say what happened?

YELLOW SHAWL. Yes! Please tell, we know so little.

BLUE BONNET. Our brother never was a writer. The last we heard from him was at the peace.

WELSHMAN. Of course. You know we tried to put to sea in January '03 but could not until February?[120] We knew something was in the offing but when we reached Gibraltar there were still no news. The Rock is a place

---

119 Similar to words found in Oldschool, 1802, 317.

120 *Naval Chronicle*, 1803, 159/160. HMS *Belleisle* (74). The *Plymouth Report* of 20 January to 17 February 1803 reported, 'Jan 23…. The Belleisle, of 84 guns… made a signal to go down the harbour, but the wind becoming scant, and rather foul, she came to at the lower moorings…. It has blown all day a hurricane… with very heavy sea in the Sound…. Feb. 10… Belleisle… weighed from Cawsand Bay, and sailed to westward'.

where gossip receives attention more than a man's victuals. The talk there was still about Saumarez off Algeciras[121] in 1800 and how in '01 some men for Jamaica[122] had mutinied for not caring to serve in such a hellish place of heat and fever.

IRISHMAN. A regiment had to be sent away[123] for want of manners.

WELSHMAN. We put back to sea before we heard about war's return. When we did hear, it was as though nature herself objected, for a volcano, Stromboli, blew its top near Sicily. We saw her leagues off and many a night she lit up the sky. We imagined a great battle took place over the horizon. A few wits worried it was a sign, but not us, nor your brother. You see, we got our new captain and Nelson was aboard the *Victory*.

WHITE GLOVES. What was Nelson like?

WELSHMAN. I'm sorry to say none of us ever met him, but we often talked about him. Anyway, we were away for months. All the way through '03 and '04 we never clapped eyes on any French warship at sea. Apart from Toulon the only land we came across was Palma and Magdalena[124] when we watered at Agincourt sound. That's on Sardinia and is a desolate and barren place where few parties go ashore for all the bandits. But at least you're safe from storms and can make repairs and get some rest. It's hard work at sea when your rigging is all rotten and your twice-laid stuff – that's old rope remade – is condemned. With all the sun, salt and heat you sweat and itch no end. Soap and linen are expensive if you can get them at all. Ain't that so, lads? We cruised endlessly and one day is like any other when there's no prize in sight. The French threatened to leave Toulon once or twice but until '05 they never did. It only changed after Spain declared war.[125]

BLUE BONNET. Is that when the chase took place?

WELSHMAN. Indeed. The French put out in January while we were at Agincourt. As soon as we heard we weighed and made the passage between Corsica and Sardinia. A difficult time it was too, for on t'other side it was foul weather. We missed the French, and Nelson reckoned they sailed for Egypt. Ships were dispatched all over the Med to find them. At Malta we

---

121 *The New American Cyclopaedia,* 1869, 362. On 6 July 1800 ships under Rear Admiral Saumarez moved against French and Spanish ships under Vice-Amiral Linois, but were beaten back. On 10 July he 'was more successful, the enemy losing 3 sail of the line, and 3,000 men killed or taken prisoners'.

122 *Cobbett's Annual Register Vol IV,* 1803, 35.

123 Lovell, 1879, 27. It went to the West Indies.

124 Maddalena.

125 12 December 1804. *Cobbett's Political Register Vol VII,* 1806, 44.

touched some merchantmen who told us the French had returned to Toulon. We had some wicked foul nights trying to double Sardinia to follow them.

ENGLISHMAN. A rough time it was.

WELSHMAN. Nelson was a sly devil. He took us to Barcelona to let French agents catch sight of us. We wanted them bold enough to put out of Toulon while we quietly sailed back that way. We met the *Phoebe*[126] who told us the French had fallen for it and put to sea. We cheered, and dutifully went south but found they had not headed that way nor towards the east. It was hard work to beat westwards for the winds were against us. Early April we heard how they had passed through the Straits. We had missed them again.

IRISHMAN. We were all made low by that.

WELSHMAN. It were a hard knock, for sure. It took us more than a fortnight to reach Gibraltar and even then we could not get inside. We had to get supplies from Barbary![127] Oh, how the purser cut up about that. The French? Well, they could have gone anywhere by then.

BLUE BONNET. They had gone to the West Indies?

WELSHMAN. The devils had indeed, along with some Spanish out of Cadiz. Eighteen sail of the line at least, and they had more than a month's start on us. But Nelson was never one to hold back and ten of us sailed in pursuit. We touched Madeira and by June were off Barbados to be told how the French were already gone to Tobago. But nothing did we see of any Frenchman there so we made for Antigua and only just missed them for a third time! They had made for home on hearing how we were after them. You see, they feared the very name of Nelson! The *Spartiate* joined us and we sailed back to the Med but sighted nothing. We were pleased to see Barbary again, for when we stood on shore for stores it was the first time for us in nearly two years.

WHITE GLOVES. You sailed all that way for nothing?

ENGLISHMAN. We helped save the Leeward and Windward Islands!

YELLOW SHAWL. So where were the French?

WELSHMAN. Rumour was they sailed to join ships out of Brest and Rochefort and made for Ireland.

IRISHMAN. Damn their eyes!

WELSHMAN. So we put out again, this time for Cape St Vincent. We did not see any ships in Cadiz and damn if we didn't also sail for Ireland!

---

126 A 36-gun frigate. See Southey, 1892, 241.
127 Tetuan.

But nothing was there so we joined Cornwallis off Ushant. Nelson went home and we returned here to refit. I don't wonder you didn't see your brother for Northumberland is such a ways off. As it turned out Admiral Calder found the enemy off Finisterre and they had put into Ferrol. But they soon got bold enough to make for Cadiz. By August it was time for Nelson to return, so we could finally deal with them.

ENGLISHMAN. Providence was on our side, for sure. We were soon back in old waters, off Cadiz. We knew it would be the main chance, as Nelson wanted to annihilate the enemy.[128] The captain told us how French ministers boasted of their 'superiority' and thought they would soon be masters of the ocean. We laughed at that and thought of prizes and glory. We danced and sang *Rule Britannia!* and *Britons, Strike Home* almost every night. You could taste victory in the air, so to speak. At least I could. But we had to coax them out by hiding over the horizon. Only a few of our frigates formed the inshore squadron to keep watch on the port and Nelson even detached some of our line ships.

WELSHMAN. Because there are always fishermen and merchantmen at sea, so the enemy knew our numbers. A few of us reckoned they had little water and supplies so would have to make for the Straits and Cartagena, or Toulon, soon enough.[129] So when they did put out we sailed after them with delight.[130] Our weather-beaten faces were full of glee! But damn, Nelson made us paint our masts and hoops yellow to make us look different to the enemy! Two days later we caught them, our twenty-seven sail of the line against thirty-three of theirs.[131] We made huzzas on deck[132] for it is we who are lords of the ocean, not them, and we readied ourselves for battle.

IRISHMAN. We weren't never going to go shy and let them roam free again! We'd sooner die.

WELSHMAN. The battle started, as they are wont to, all slow and deliberate. There was little wind and we had studding sails on both sides.

---

128 *The Annual Register*, 1834, 430. It states his letters 'show how completely his mind was occupied with but one desire, one hope – that the enemy might come out and meet annihilation'.

129 Butler, 1819, 354.

130 *The Christmas Tribute*, 1851, 236. From a long piece titled 'The Battle of Trafalgar, by a Young Officer' that stated how Nelson ordered the painting of the masts and hoops of the *Belleisle*; the crew 'rushing up the hatchways to get a glimpse of the hostile fleet'; the officers at breakfast on the fateful day and the results of the battering the ship took in the battle.

131 *The British Navy Triumphant*, 1805, 31.

132 Worsley, 1808, 5.

We wet and covered our decks with sand, filled buckets with water and rigged fire screens.[133] As we closed them, both Irish and I went below on the lookout for leaks. That's what carpenter's-mates' assistants do, see.[134] We creep along the ribs of the ship hoping never to see water that's not in the well. Especially if a ship leaks no end.

ENGLISHMAN. I went with the boatswain to keep an eye on the rigging.[135]

WELSHMAN. Everyone has a role in battle. Lieutenants attend the batteries, the master commands the ship and sails, the gunner and carpenter go wherever necessary, the marines position themselves around the ship and often at the great guns. Your brother went with the master. All that Irish and I could tell after that was what a few others told us later. You don't see much below.

ENGLISHMAN. I got to see the enemy hoist their colours when their guns opened up on us with an awful noise. One man near to me lost his head.

WHITE GLOVES. He went mad?

ENGLISHMAN. No, miss. His head was… well, he died. Our captain was also hit, I saw that too. We were all told to fall to the deck but I were already there. As we passed one Spanish ship – the *Santa Ana* I think – we opened up on her but soon lost our top masts and sails by the board. I was ordered to man a gun not screened by them. We got close enough that our muzzles touched theirs! I was all handsome at first, although I thought I would suffocate from the smoke, and then a splinter knocked me senseless. When I came to I was covered in blood from my ears. I knew we had passed the Spanish ship as we then had a Frenchie on either side and another one raked us something cruel. I saw them through the ruin of our gun ports, see. The enemy crowded all round, and I couldn't make head nor tail of our own ships. We were quite alone. Then our main mast fell.

IRISHMAN. We felt it go. A great shudder.

WELSHMAN. It nearly stove us through and if it had we'd have all gone down. We were nought but a hulk by then.

WHITE GLOVES. Was there… much blood?

ENGLISHMAN. Spill a pint of spirits upon the floor and you'll see the puddle it makes, miss. Dozens of men drained of their life-blood on deck? Without masts you roll with the swell. Ever seen a sluice?

---

133 Used to stop fire spreading. See Steel, P., 1804, 15.

134 A first and second rate carried two carpenter's mates. A third rate carried one with eight assistants. *Encyclopaedia Britannica*, 1810, under RAT.

135 Steel, 1790, 39.

WELSHMAN. Perhaps we should say no more.

ENGLISHMAN. Hmm. Well, those who could cut up a caper did so, as the *Swiftsure*[136] approached. We needed her aid by then.

WELSHMAN. We heard the hullabaloo below and joined in. The battle was over. For four hours we had been at it. So we made our reports and went to the gunroom to say farewell to the fallen. A few were there waiting on the surgeon. It felt strangely quiet, I can tell you.

BLUE BONNET. You saw our brother?

WELSHMAN. He… had already been consigned to the deep, miss.

WHITE GLOVES. How many died?

WELSHMAN. Thirty-three. More than ninety were wounded.

BLUE BONNET. When they were buried, was it a nice service?

IRISHMAN. It were.[137]

YELLOW SHAWL. Our brother would have liked that.

WELSHMAN. We were a red wreck and had to be towed to Gibraltar for repair before we could sail home. And that's it, all told. We're sorry for your loss, ladies. Know that your brother died bravely in service of his king and country.

BLUE BONNET. Thank you, we are grateful for your sentiments. You did your duty and make us proud of your skill and bravery. But now I think we should take some tea? I believe they make scones in the inn over there.

The sailors who met the three sisters of their dead friend were not unusual, for apart from a few senior officers and those on deck most of a ship's complement would have been busy with sails, ropes, guns or other duties below decks. Reports had to be written shortly afterwards, sometimes by distant observers upon repeating frigates[138] or vessels, or written up as a dispatch or memoir. The exception was if a battle or engagement took place close enough to shore to be observed from there. For instance, 'M. Denon was an eye-witness of the battle of the Nile, from a tower in the neighbourhood of the Bay of Aboukir.'[139] The final butcher's bill of dead and wounded, and formulaic entries in ships' logs, never gave a true account of what took place. Every battle, if a man or woman survived, was a personal affair unique to themselves. With the arrival of the peace of Amiens it would have been assumed by many naval personnel that they would never experience a sea battle again.

---

136 *The Christmas Tribute, ibid,* 244.
137 One sailor was found to be still alive when about to be thrown overboard.
138 Ships stationed out of the line of battle to repeat the flagship's signals.
139 *Naval Chronicle Vol IX,* 1803, 475.

However, by late 1802 it was apparent that France remained emboldened and had continued to encroach upon others. She secretly regained control of Louisiana, openly sent troops to Saint-Domingue and Pondichéry (which were her own colonies after all), retained troops in the Batavian Republic, annexed Piedmont and interfered in Swiss affairs. Bonaparte ridiculed British alarm over Piedmont as 'mere trifles',[140] but Louisiana particularly worried London because 'The possession of these countries, and of course the Mississippi, by the French, will place that nation in a situation to annoy, if not endanger, the British possessions in the West Indies.'[141] 'La Nouvelle-Orléans' increased French economic power in the region and gave access to a wealth of stores and goods. It also worried the United States of America who believed France had also gained possession of the Floridas.

In turn Britain dragged her heels over Malta and the Cape of Good Hope. The British felt the need to balance peace and her influence, all the while being mindful of the French. Valletta, the main port of Malta, was a harbour both parliament and the Navy were loath to give up. 'No cession made by the treaty had been more generally lamented by Englishmen, keenly sensitive to all that affected their position in the Mediterranean or threatened the approach to India'.[142] Troops were kept at the Cape while France delayed her evacuation of Holland.

A tense situation existed when, on 30 January 1803, a report by Colonel Horace François Bastien Sébastiani de La Porta was published in the French paper *Moniteur*.[143] It laid out the situation in the eastern Mediterranean and concluded that a few thousand French troops was all that was required to wrest control of both Egypt and the Ionian islands.[144] It caused anger and alarm in London. Some British politicians believed that at the very least the report aimed to pressure Britain to quit Malta, or else it had been designed to provoke a 'maritime war'[145] and allow Napoléon to extricate himself from a difficult situation on Saint-Domingue. According to the French historian and statesman Adolphe Thiers, men like 'Wyndham, Dundas [and] Grenville, raised a greater outcry than ever, and drowned the voices of the liberal men, such as Mr. Fox and his friends.'[146]

---

140 Coote, 1817, 22.
141 See Webster, 1802, 225. Louisiana was sold to the USA on 30 April 1803.
142 Mahan, 1902, 121.
143 Thiers, 1893, 482.
144 Scott, 1887, 325.
145 Mahan, *ibid,* 94.
146 Thiers, *ibid,* 483.

The British government offered Elba to France with recognition of French controlled Etruria, all in exchange for Malta[147] but nothing came of it. On 8 March 1803 a public message from King George was proclaimed in the Imperial Parliament which stated that as France and Holland were making military preparations he 'judged it expedient to adopt additional measures of precaution for the security for his dominions'.[148] Whereas he wished the continuance of peace he desired a 'public spirit' to enable him to 'adopt such measures as circumstances may appear to require'.[149] This stung Bonaparte, who had a public confrontation with the British ambassador, Lord Charles Whitworth, on 13 March 1803 to whom he bluntly asked, 'Why these armaments?... . I have not a single ship of the line in the ports of France; but if you wish to arm, I will arm also: if you wish to fight, I will fight also.'[150]

Britain could never hope to best her enemy on land. It was felt by many that the strength of the nation was gained through trade and sea commerce, and that the navy was the guarantor. Both the merchant navy and the Royal Navy were mutually connected and it was superiority at sea, rather than maintenance of a strong landed army, that guaranteed liberty.[151] This had been written about by Edmund Burke in the first ever *Annual Register* of 1758 when he had mentioned three factions then contending for power in Britain, of which the most popular faction believed that 'a standing army is, in whatever shape, dangerous to freedom' and much preferred a strong navy. As an island nation with a small population the kingdom needed her senior service, with the assistance of an army, to protect her interests and conduct a war.

The 'Plymouth Report' of 20 February to 22 March 1803 shows clearly the effect the king's message, and eventual declaration of war, had upon all naval ports. Just before the arrival of the message it was simple administration of naval lieutenants and how they were to be examined[152] 'in England... by the Commissioners of His Majesty's Navy at Somerset House';[153] recruitment of volunteers to man the *Courageux* (74), *Boadicea* (44), *Nemesis* (32), and the 14s *Atalante, Escort* and *Rambler*; and completion of the rigging for

---

147 Burke, 1805, 710.
148 *Naval Chronicle Vol IX*, 1803, 225.
149 *Naval Chronicle Vol IX*, ibid.
150 Goldsmith, 1823, 455.
151 Burke, 1795, 12.
152 For a naval lieutenant to be 'passed' he had to be examined; traditionally in London, but widened to naval ports due to the expansion of the fleets.
153 *Naval Chronicle*, 1803, 242. This did not extend to India and the Cape.

the *Plantagenet* (74), then alongside the *Yarmouth* hulk in the Hamoaze, so as to put her in commission. Her captain was the son of the comptroller of the navy.

A message could have been forwarded by telegraph from London to Plymouth in twenty-two minutes[154] but this would have been intercepted. On 10 March 1803 the port admiral, Rear Admiral Dacres, received communications rushed down from London, in thirty-two hours, of an additional 10,000 men voted by Parliament for the navy together with sealed orders. Thereafter things changed. The barracks at Stonehouse and Mill Bay were shut to the public. 'About 7 P.M. the town was alarmed with the marching of several bodies of Royal Marines… armed towards the Quays.'[155] A few files of men marched inland to Dartmouth and Modbury, and roads in and out of Plymouth were sealed. Royal Marines boarded colliers at New Quay near to Batter Street, ships in the Cattewater, the Pool and elsewhere. Sailors were hauled out of gin shops and sent on board the flagship, while landmen of all descriptions were pressed anywhere they were found. 'The town looked as if in a state of siege.' One press gang 'entered the Dock Theatre, and cleared the whole gallery, except the women.' Some men managed to hide but were taken the following day in lodgings 'discovered by their girls'. A few who had hidden in marble quarries outside the town were later apprehended and pressed for the *Culloden* (74). More than 600 men suddenly found themselves thrown into another war. On 11 March 1803 Viscount Sidmouth reported, 'We are happy to learn that the alacrity with which seamen re-enter the service is absolutely without example. This is, indeed, a genuine proof of British spirit!'[156]

The *Gannet* (14) put to sea with dispatches for the West Indies, the 14s *Eagle* and *Ranger* set out on a cruise against smugglers, the *Acasta* (40) departed to procure sailors at Guernsey. Orders were given to put in to commission the *Malta* (84), and the 74s *Conquerant*, *Spencer*, *Spartiate* and *Mars* then idle in the Hamoaze. Contracts were made to convey large amounts of wheat for the baking of biscuit at the Victualling Office and extra bakers were recruited. Dock visibly increased in activity as it was a rush to get ships to sea. Bad weather caused some problems, for the Sound was always open to the ravages of the weather, and a whole fleet of French fishing boats suddenly sought shelter. Over the next few days

---

154 Warner, 1808, 62. Also called the semaphore. An electrical version was offered to the admiralty in 1816.

155 *Naval Chronicle, ibid*, 243. Other details from this source.

156 *Cobbett's Parliamentary Debates Vol III*, 1803, 699.

various warships arrived from around Britain. Revenue cutters were placed under command of the port admiral. Press gangs fanned out towards the east to find ever more men, although 'Upon a survey of all the impressed men before three Captains and three Surgeons of the Royal Navy, such as were deemed unfit for His Majesty's service, as well as apprentices, were immediately discharged.'[157]

Admiral Keith arrived to superintend the fitting out of the fleet. Sailors were taken from ships in ordinary to help rig commissioned warships. One vessel arrived with news of warlike preparations at Cherbourg. Plymouth was soon swept clean of men so warships had to put out for other British ports to complete their complements and build the wooden wall. Squadrons formed up to either blockade Brest and Toulon or patrol all the seas around Britain. And so on. A fever of activity and a fervid sense of purpose was released: men had to be recruited, ships brought into commission, stores and armaments gathered. It was once more unto the breach, dear friends, once more.

Not everyone was convinced all went well. A letter dated 10 April 1803 appeared in *Cobbett's Annual Register*. Written by 'An Englishman' from Plymouth it complained, 'Six weeks have now nearly elapsed since his Majesty's Message... and we may naturally suppose, that the state of things, which led to that Message being sent, was such, that the ministers, and amongst them, the First Lord of the Admiralty, must have seen, that it was possible such a crisis might arise, and, in consequence, that he would have taken every step that could be taken, (without suspicion or alarm) towards preparation for it; but so far... the scene of hurry, confusion, contradictory orders, and total want of system, that has been exhibited since the evil took place... has been in proportion to the ignorance, arrogance, and presumption of those who preside at and manage the naval department.'[158]

'An Englishman' argued that partiality and arbitrary conduct had weakened the navy. It was known that there had been a 'deficiency of workmen and of materials... [that caused] a suspension in the routine of dock-yard business. New ships could not be built; nor, and a very serious misfortune it was, could old ones be repaired. Many of the ships in commission, too, having been merely patched up, were scarcely in a state to keep the sea.'[159] The naval superpower's crown seems to have been dented but William James, who wrote after the era had closed, considered that

---

157 *Naval Chronicle, ibid*, 244.
158 *Cobbett's Annual Register*, 1803, 646/7.
159 James, Vol III, 310.

whereas St Vincent's investigation into peculation and embezzlement may have done temporary harm it bequeathed long term benefits.

The United Kingdom of Great Britain and Ireland formally declared war on France on 18 May 1803.

Already set for the year was an estimate of 50,000 men including 12,000 Royal Marines, added to on 14 March by 10,000 additional men 'for the sea service', and a 'further additional number of 40,000 men... including 8,000 royal marines' in June with 'Total supplies for the navy, for 1803... [of] £10,211,378.13.1'.[160] Estimates had to be made to provide enough manpower to allow fleets to cover home and distant waters but the situation in the West Indies was immeasurably improved upon when France sold Louisiana to the United States of America a little over a month into the new conflict.

Thomas Paine wrote *A Letter To The English People on the Invasion of England*[161] in 1804 that stated, 'We see England almost perpetually in war, or warlike disputes, and her debt and taxes continually increasing.' He thought England (that is, the United Kingdom) to be 'eccentric and wild' who since the American War had had disputes with Holland, Russia, Spain and France and had 'declared war again to avoid fulfilling the treaty' with her refusal to evacuate Malta. He believed that Britain's declaration of war 'was the same as sending a challenge to Bonaparte to invade England and make it the seat of war'. England went to war, he thought, to protect her commerce but she had made an error in her refusal to depart Malta.

Two years later, in 1806, a rather large amateur poet and his even larger wife toured Plymouth to visit scenes of naval endeavour. They walked through Dock, East Stonehouse and ended their first day upon the walls of the citadel (having written for permission to do so). Up against a parapet they took in a most splendid view. Their guide – one of the invalids who manned the place – tried to point out the bastions, curtains, ravelins, horn-work, counterscarp and covered way of the citadel but it was Plymouth far below them, the Hoe, Mount Wise, the entrance to the Tamar, Mount Edgcumbe woods, Maker Tower, the vast Sound and Channel with distant Eddystone[162] on the horizon, the river Plym, Saltram on her banks and the dun coloured hills of Dartmoor beyond that held their attention. The poet had grown up in Plymouth but had moved to Leicester as a young man. He felt good to be back, if only for a short time. As a poet the muse

---

160 Campbell, Berkenhout et al, 1817, 2-4.
161 Paine, 1817, 4. Other Paine quotes from this source.
162 With its lighthouse.

often stirred within him and silently he began to form phrases in his mind. *Drake's island with battery and furnace so warm, To deter the enemy if they ever dared swarm* – but he could not finish, for the guide moved them on.

Despite their long journey down country the stout poet easily persuaded his wife to join him, for the thought of scalded cream[163] and bracing sea air to aide her rheumatism hit the mark. It was very much a tour of destiny for the poet. Infused with the splendour of a strong naval presence and fulsome British sailors on show he had high hopes to pen an epic ode about Trafalgar, publish it himself and make his name and fortune. Odes and poems were very popular at this time.

Back in their room at the King's Arms,[164] his wife snoring on the bed, the poet took paper and quill and readied himself to receive inspiration. But nothing came. So he opened his notebook to those pages dated 1803. He recalled how, during the peace, many people had hoped to avoid a war with France but war came nonetheless, and Nelson had boarded the *Victory* at Portsmouth on 18 May 1803 to sail to the Mediterranean. *Our defiant hero set forth to war, His destiny to be remembered forever more. His nation could not forego, Her navy to best the foe.* It was no good, he needed some fresh air.

As he sauntered through the inn a further flight of images came to mind of how, between war's return and Nelson's last battle, the nation had trembled with the threat of another invasion. Flat-boats from the previous conflict resided along the enemy channel coast and France had strengthened her shore defences.[165] The period from 1803 until late 1805 it was ultimately 'a striking and wonderful pause in the world's history'[166] but the Royal Navy could not know that and had had to account for all possible outcomes. Due to the nature of the French channel coast, few ports could assume the role of departure point for the transports required for an invasion flotilla, but they did allow for small boats to steal along the coast. 'No vessel, indeed, beyond a gun-brig in size, can approach near enough to do any execution.'[167] Boulogne was the chosen place of rendezvous and by a loose concentration

---

163 Or clotted cream. Urban, 1791, 720.

164 Cary, 1802, 77

165 She squandered her resources on these flotillas at the expense of her navy. Mahan, *ibid*, 107.

166 *Ibid*, 117.

167 James, Vol III, 317. The term 'chosen place of rendezvous' found in the *The Annual Register*, 1807, 134.

of force outside that harbour the Royal Navy harried the flats, prams[168] and gun-vessels. The British knew they would do great damage to the French even before they could arrive off the English coast.

For France, to land troops in large numbers would have been difficult if not impossible, but nonetheless she doggedly built up her invasion force. By 1805 Boulogne 'sheltered over a thousand gunboats and transports ready to carry forty thousand men to the shores of England. North and south, not only the neighbourhood of the harbour but the whole coast bristled with cannon, and opposite the entrance rose a powerful work, built upon piles, to protect the vessels when going out and also when anchored outside... . [but] So many boats could not pass out through the narrow channel during one high water.'[169] French troops that assembled for the attempt continually practiced embarkation and landing. 'And the eyes of all Europe were directed towards the preparations for an achievement, on the event of which the fate not only of the two countries was at issue, but that also of the whole moral and political world.'[170]

Nearby French ports held smaller concentrations of gunboats and transports for men and horses. But it would have required two days to allow them all out, due to the tides, giving ample opportunity for the British to attack the first tier that dared leave. It required a British squadron large enough to deal with enemy warships and powerful shore defences, for once outside the protection of French harbours enemy flats would undoubtedly have hugged the coast. The French knew this and a possible alternative was to use boats propelled by oars, but this necessitated fog to allow time to make the passage across the channel. British squadrons only had to observe the weather for those rare days when the French could have put forth. If the French had managed to reach England, a number of gun-vessels, militia, and army regiments awaited them. And the surf would have had to be suitable to land so many.

The question at the time was whether the invasion would ever take place. Britain could not assume it would not, nor that the invasion flotilla would not receive cover of a powerful fleet. Enemy line of battleships were assembled and strengthened in various ports. Which is why British admirals ventured far and wide. Nelson kept watch on Toulon. Admiral Cornwallis eventually put out from Cawsand 'with a fleet of 100 sail of the line and

---

168 A pram, or prame, carried twelve 24-pounders and around 100 troops. 'A kind of floating battery' – *A Military and Naval Encyclopaedia*, 1879, 953.

169 Mahan, *ibid*, 114/115.

170 *The Annual Register*, ibid, 134.

frigates',[171] his flag aboard the *Dreadnought* (98) but soon shifted to the *Ville-de-Paris* (112), to take station off Ushant and Brest. Rear Admiral Collingwood[172] patrolled off Brest and Rochefort.[173] Rear Admiral Pellew was soon off Ferrol.[174] With such a small naval threat posed by the Batavian republic, Royal Navy squadrons ranged along the entire channel and into the North Sea.

Britain and her naval enemies were like prizefighters ready to enter the ring. However, many British ships were not fit for sea. William James later maintained that if only ten had been useful, the French were not in a state to counter them, although they soon launched two new 74s, the *Cassard* and the *Vengeur.* Such considerations were far below the purview of the poet who only imagined thousands of sailors expectant of battle, the drum beating them to quarters. *Drake's drum starts to beat, But never for mercy does it entreat, Victory is certain, Victory is ours, While our ships are worked by good British tars!*

Outside with pencil and notebook in hand the rhymester walked familiar narrow streets, steep and somewhat dingy with open sewers, down to Sutton Pool. So much history was on show. He had to stop occasionally to catch his breath and turn a page or two. His notes reminded him how Mr Pitt, on 15 March 1804, criticised the Navy for not having been ready. The Admiralty, he said, had not 'made sufficient provision either for the present or future existence of the navy'.[175] The venerable member had argued there was a far inferior number of gunboats to repel the enemy than had been 'at any period in former times'.[176] He believed 'Gross neglect' had been committed, while France's 'Squadron of the North' was to have ten 74s built to strengthen it further, and Brest held twenty-one serviceable line ships.[177]

The British sea service could only watch and wait for the supposed great attempt, while contenting itself with harassing the French as much as possible. In truth it was made a disgruntled behemoth swatting at gnats. With years of experience of blockade, bombardment, and cutting outs at least this came quite naturally, but some complained how Earl St Vincent had alienated so many within British yards it had created an inability to

171 James, *ibid*, 255.
172 Promoted to vice admiral 1804.
173 He was there by November 1804. Newnham Collingwood, 1828, 132.
174 See letters contained in *Papers Relative to the Discussion with Spain in 1802, 1803, and 1804*, 1805, 343-6.
175 *An Answer to Mr. Pitt's Attack upon Earl St. Vincent,* 1804, 48.
176 *An Answer to Mr. Pitt's Attack, ibid*, 288.
177 James, Vol III, 253.

strengthen and sustain the fleets. With war's return the senior service was expected to do it all over again with only 67 ships of the line, 249 gunships, frigates and sloops and precious few others[178] while the French had on her stocks at home and abroad 66 line of battle ships and frigates.[179]

But time revealed France's navy was not ready and the British government underwent a change with the return of Pitt and his second ministry. Viscount Melville was made the First Lord of the Admiralty until May 1805 when he was removed due to his impending impeachment and Charles Middleton, Baron Barham, became his successor. After the removal of Earl St Vincent the Navy began to rebuild her strength. On 14 May 1806 it was reported to Parliament, '42 ships of the line and 45 frigates, had been launched between 1783 and 1792... . That from Jan. 1793, to Feb. 1801, there were 18 ships of the line, and 46 frigates built... That on 18th Feb, 1801, when the earl of St. Vincent came into office, there were building, 15 sail of the line... and 11 frigates... . That between the 18th Feb. 1801, and the 15th May 1804, there were launched [10] sail of the line, and [12] frigates.'[180] Twenty-two ships were launched before Trafalgar. *Ne'er a sword could France draw upon England's blessed shore, They strove in vain for Britain ruled the deep blue main.*

Amongst the many merchant ships at Sutton Pool, which was a scene of awful impressment in recent times, the portly poet looked out to the Cattewater and Mount Batten Point. To his right the citadel loomed high above and within its long shadow, all the way to Fisher's Point, stood the victualling offices in full flow. Through the gate[181] he saw shutes conveying flour to the bakehouse and he could almost taste the biscuits, imprinted with a broad arrow and the words PLY, that poured continually out of eight ovens. It was loud and dusty, for enough was made to feed thousands of sailors. It made him hungry so despite the late evening he bought some Saltash oysters from an evil looking oyster-wench and sat on an upturned barrel to devour them. There he remained afterwards to read his little book.

From mid-1803 until Trafalgar it was mostly the lull and boredom of blockade, occasional small actions between frigates and vessels, and bombardment of French coastal towns. On 2 October 1804 a number of fire vessels (called catamarans) were cut from launches and allowed to drift into Boulogne. Some thought them to be quackery and innovation and although

---

178 Derrick, 1806, 218.
179 James, *ibid*, 245.
180 See *The Parliamentary Debates*, 1812, 186/7.
181 Britton and Brayley, 1803, 143; and *The Picture of Plymouth*, 1812, 70.

they caused the French some alarm they had little effect. The poet's little book reminded him how each vessel had received a name, such as *Peggy, Devonshire,* and *Providence.*

By 1 October 1805 the Navy had climbed to a strength of around 124 ships of the line, 158 frigates and 416 other vessels for a total of 698 commissioned ships.[182] The abstract for 1806 showed that an exceptional number of ships of war had been ordered to be built in the previous year. One was the first ever British naval warship constructed from teak, and William James later laid out those ships by name which had been strengthened or sheathed in the same period. There were three 98s, two 80s, twelve 74s, five 64s, three 38s, two 36s and six 12s.[183] It was a colossal undertaking and demonstrated both the worry of the threat of invasion and the energy unleashed under the new administration.

By late 1804 the French invasion army approached 160,000 men and communes funded one vessel each for the enterprise. The French navy became motivated to a level far beyond anything it had managed in the previous war. France controlled, directly or indirectly, most of Europe's western coastline and with Spain's declaration of war on 12 December 1804 she also gained access to Spanish ports. However, until 1805 she remained distracted and her European based fleets never really ventured out to sea.

The poet felt a gripe in his guts so made his ponderous way back to the inn. He felt decidedly queasy. The crooked streets darkened and a few rough types began to appear.

1805 was a pivotal year. Paris and Madrid had hoped to gather 30,000 men at the Texel, 120,000 around Boulogne, 25,000 at Brest, 4,000 at Rochefort, 9,000 at Toulon, 5,000 Spanish and 20,000 French at Cadiz for more than 200,000 men for the invasion of Britain.[184] Bonaparte's navy commanded a potential force of 70 sail of the line opposed to 83 serviceable British sail of the line.[185] With spies and agents and printed material, each side well knew the size of each other's navies. It was a close call, but despite a contraction in ships the Royal Navy remained a force to be reckoned with.

The poet arrived back at the inn with his face bathed in sweat and his stomach in torment. The privy was reached only just in time.

---

182 Derrick, *ibid*, 227. He also stated different numbers at the start of 1805: 177 line ships and a combined total of 770. Other sources give 175 and 949 in total. All of these sources, although not in full agreement, include harbour ships etc.

183 James, 1824, 2 and 3.

184 James, *ibid*, 431.

185 James, *ibid*. He reckoned Britain had 105 sail of the line, of which 83 were serviceable.

For almost two years the senior service fulfilled its role in all weathers and even managed to better the gap in ships between herself and her combined enemies. But she was ever half-blind to what her foes planned. Napoléon desired his Brest fleet to sail to the West Indies then return home to deliver the final blow. This fleet was to unite with a combined force of ships out of Rochefort and Ferrol, and various plans were formulated as to how this would take place. The press published misleading reports to confuse the British. All the Royal Navy could do was pursue her own duties until Nelson embarked upon his great chase. *To the amethyst waters of Tobago he sailed, The Leewards and Windwards no longer imperilled, To Ireland and Ushant far did he roam, Until relieved when he returned home.*

However, as Nelson pursued the combined fleet across the Atlantic the situation in Europe altered. On 11 April 1805 Britain made a concert with Russia to 'collect together a force which, independently of the succours furnished by his Britannic majesty, might amount to 500,000 effective men... to induce or compel the French government to consent to the re-establishment of peace, and of the balance of Europe'.[186] They agreed to the re-establishment of the king of Sardinia in Piedmont, security for Naples, independence of Holland and Switzerland and a 'solid barrier against future usurpations'. Britain offered further subsidies and transports for troops. After Bonaparte annexed Genoa it brought Austria to the league on 9 August 1805.[187] Russia marched two armies to the Danube, stating they were merely an aide for negotiations of a possible peace, and everything was seen as a direct threat to the French. Napoléon resolved to reply by the one means he could. He marched his entire force against this 'combination'. He reinforced his army in Italy, ordered troops for the invasion of England to disband, and marched his armies in Holland and Hanover towards the Danube. The invasion threat of England was ended.

Back at his desk, his wife awake but drowsy, the poet re-ordered his notes in the vain hope he would receive inspiration. He read how large crowds had gathered to see Nelson rejoin the *Victory* and depart England for the last time.[188] He 'sailed from St. Helen's... with the Euryalus frigate, on the morning of the 15th of September 1805... . On the 18th he appeared off Plymouth.'[189] By the end of September he was off Cadiz. But would the enemy put to sea?

---

186 *The Annual Register,* ibid, 139.
187 *The Annual Register,* ibid, 139. This same source considered that British ministers, or councils, 'were void of judgment, foresight, and activity'.
188 14 September 1805.
189 Beatty, 1807, 1.

Fate intervened. In Cadiz the French admiral, Villeneuve, found himself in a difficult situation. The Spanish were sarcastic of recent decisions he had made. His conduct was written about in the *Moniteur*,[190] and he had been told he was to be replaced. So on 19 October 1805 he put to sea with the Spanish under admiral Gravina. Did he hope to restore his reputation? It was assumed by the British that this combined fleet was for the Mediterranean so they made all sail in pursuit.[191] Two days later, seven leagues off Cape Trafalgar, the British closed in two columns in very light winds against the enemy that had formed up in an irregular line which convexed as a crescent to leeward. Villeneuve had previously decided to attack in the usual line of battle.

The poet had details of all the ships that took part that fateful day. The British van, or weather column, comprised[192] the 100s *Britannia* and *Victory*; the 98s *Neptune* and *Téméraire*; the 74s *Ajax, Conqueror, Leviathan, Minotaur, Orion* and *Spartiate*; the 64s *Africa* and *Agamemnon; Naiad* (38), the 36s *Euryalus, Phoebe,* and *Sirius; Pickle* (10); and the cutter *Entreprenante.* The rear, or lee column, comprised the *Royal Sovereign* (100); the 98s *Dreadnought* and *Prince; Tonnant* (80); the 74s *Achille, Belleisle, Bellerophon, Colossus, Defence, Defiance, Mars, Revenge, Swiftsure* and *Thunderer*; and the *Polyphemus* (64). The British plan of attack had likewise been fixed upon and Nelson had previously stated, 'In case signals cannot be seen or clearly understood, no captain can do wrong if he places his ship alongside that of an enemy.'[193]

The combined enemy fleet comprised 18 French and 15 Spanish ships. There was the *Nuestra Señora de la Santísima Trinidad* (136); the 112s *Principe de Asturias* (Almirante Gravina) and *Santa Ana*; the *Rayo* (100); the 80s *Argonauta, Bucentaure* (Amiral Villeneuve), *Formidable, Indomptable, Neptune* and *Neptuno*; the 74s *Achille, Aigle, Algésiras, Argonaute, Bahama, Berwick, Duguay Trouin, Fougueux, Héros, Intrépide, Monarca, Montañés, Mont Blanc, Pluton, Redoubtable, San Augustine, San Francisco de Asis, San Ildefonso, San Juan Nepomuceno, San Justo, Scipion* and *Swiftsure*; the *San Leandro* (64); the 40s *Cornélie, Hermione, Hortense, Rhin* and *Thémis*; the 18s *Argus* and *Furet.*

---

190 *The Annual Register,* ibid, 234.
191 From dispatches from Vice Admiral Collingwood. See *The British Navy Triumphant!*, 1805, 30.
192 But not in the order shown. *The British Navy Triumphant!*, 1805, 34. Likewise the French and Spanish. See map for the actual positions of ships.
193 *Naval Chronicle Vol XIV*, 1805, 504.

So many ships, the poet wondered. So much assured death and destruction. *Eager British ships made sail for their foe, To halt their designs and bring them woe, French and Spanish hopes halted and checked, Their ships captured, burnt, or made pitiful wrecks.*

The battle opened at a stately pace and Nelson appeared on deck 'dressed as usual in his admiral's frock-coat, bearing on his left breast four stars of different orders, which he always wore with his common apparel.... [but] This was the only action in which he ever appeared without a sword.'[194] His flagship lead his column (the *Téméraire* had wanted to) and twenty minutes before noon the vice admiral ordered the following signal be hoisted: 'England confides that every man will do his duty.' The signal-lieutenant, John Pascoe, was unable to replicate the word 'confides' so offered a substitute of 'expects'. Nelson agreed and this famous naval signal was hoisted.

Vice Admiral Collingwood, in command of the lee column on the *Royal Sovereign*, wrote in his dispatch of 22 October that 'in leading down to their centre, I had both their van and rear abaft the beam.'[195] As he approached the enemy, the *Santa Ana* fired on him as he passed her stern. The *Belleisle* and *Mars* likewise engaged, while the *Victory* made for the *Nuestra Señora de la Santísima Trinidad*. Collingwood broke the enemy line 'about the twelfth ship from the rear' while Nelson broke the line 'about the tenth from the van'.[196] He had intended to penetrate 'the adversary's line, between the tenth and eleventh of his ships in the van; but finding it so close, that there was not room to pass, he ordered the Victory... to be run on board the ship opposed to him.'[197] The enemy was left with 'fourteen ships in the van, and nineteen in the rear division, with a space of nearly a mile between them'.[198] Ships engaged in general action at the 'muzzles of their guns'.

The consequent carnage was terrible. All the *Belleisle*'s masts went by the board and her sails covered most of her guns. The *Victory* had her mizzen-topmast, studding sails and booms shot away. She was 'laid aboard' the *Redoubtable*, which ship had the *Téméraire* alongside her opposite side, while the *Téméraire* suffered the *Fougueux* on her opposite side. Four ships found themselves aboard each other.[199]

---

194 Allen, 1853, 217.
195 *The British Navy Triumphant*, 1805, 31.
196 *Ibid*, 31.
197 *The Annual Register*, 1807, 235.
198 Allen, *ibid*, 220.
199 Ekins, 1824, 269.

Nelson, who refused to hide his 'insignia', was an open and visible target to 'musketeers in the tops of the enemy's ships'.[200] A *musket* ball hit him in the left breast and he died after two hours. By three o'clock twenty-one enemy ships had either struck their colours, sunk, or burned.[201] Almirante Gravina had to stand in towards Cadiz with some of his ships but the British captured nineteen ships of the line. The *Achille* (74) blew up, but some 200 of her crew were saved by tenders. A young officer later wrote of what happened on the *Belleisle* and said, 'The view of the fleet at this period was highly interesting, and would have formed a beautiful subject for a painter. Just under the setting rays were five or six dismantled prizes: on one hand lay the Victory, with part of our fleet and prizes; and on the left hand the Sovereign and a similar cluster of ships. The remnant of the combined fleet was making for Cadiz... . The Achille had burnt to the water's edge, with the tri-coloured ensign still displayed, about a mile from us, and our tenders and boats were using every effort to save the brave fellows.'[202]

Of the thirty-three ships of the combined squadron sixteen were 'destroyed, four were carried to Gibraltar, six escaped into Cadiz, mere wrecks, and four which retired from the action, were 13 days after captured.'[203] Those ships captured were *Bahama, San Ildefonso, San Juan Nepomuceno* and *Swiftsure*. Ships wrecked were *Achille, Argonaute, Berwick, Bucentaur, Fougueux* (all men perished), *Indomptable* (all men perished), *Intrépide, l'Aigle, Monarca, Neptuno, Rayo, San Augustine* and *San Francisco de Asis*. Ships sunk were *Argonauta, Nuestra Señora de la Santísima Trinidad* and *Redoubtable*. Those that escaped were *Duguay Trouin, Formidable, Mont Blanc* and *Scipion*.[204] So damaged was the *Royal Sovereign* that Collingwood had to remove himself to the *Euryalus*. The British afterwards found themselves in a dire situation for many ships had been dismasted and the 'shoals of Trafalgar' were perilously near as a gale arrived. Seven years later Sir John Carr could write that 'several pieces of wrecks are to be found upon the beach.'[205]

The poet's wife was used to her husband shedding a tear now and then. He was, she thought, far too sensitive for his own good. As he sat hunched over the desk, no doubt sobbing, she got undressed and went to sleep. In his

---

200 Lemprière, 1808, under NEL.
201 Derrick, 1806, 229.
202 *The Christmas Tribute*, ibid, 244.
203 Lemprière, *ibid*.
204 Urban, 1805, 1159.
205 *Select Reviews of Literature*, 1812, 334.

left hand the poet held a facsimile of Vice Admiral Collingwood's despatch. It talked of the 'valour and skill which were displayed by the Officers, the Seamen, and Marines, in the battle with the enemy, where every individual appeared an hero… a brilliant instance of what Britons can do, when their King and their country need their service.'[206] The *Victory* had been typical of the dead and wounded. Along with Nelson those who died were Captain (Royal Marines) Charles Adair, Lieutenant W. Ram, midshipmen Rob. Smith and Alex. Palmer, a secretary and the captain's clerk. Amongst the wounded were two naval lieutenants and two lieutenants (Royal Marines), two midshipmen and one agent victualler's clerk.

The *Belleisle* lost '2 officers, 1 petty officer, 22 seamen, and 8 marines, killed; 3 officers, 3 petty officers, 68 seamen, and 19 marines wounded'.[207] Those named who died were lieutenants Ebenezer Geall and John Woodin, midshipman George Nind; those named as wounded were lieutenant W. Ferrie, and lieutenant (Royal Marines) Jn. Owen, boatswain Andrew Gibson, master's mates W.H. Pearson and W. Culfield, midshipman Sam. Jago and volunteer first class J.T. Hodge.

Combined the British lost 21 officers, 15 petty officers, 283 seamen and 104 royal marines killed with 41 officers, 57 petty officers, 870 seamen, and 196 royal marines wounded.[208] 'Of the three commanders in chief… not one remained alive twelve months afterwards.'[209] Nelson passed away on the day of battle, Almirante Don Federico Carlos Gravina y Nápoli a few months later. Amiral Villeneuve died in 1806 (stabbed numerous times but reported by the French as a suicide).

As night deepened the poet was on the verge of giving up as none of his ideas found any form. He struggled to suggest why Trafalgar had been a happy time and so celebrated on a national scale. The French invasion of Britain had already been called off so the mood ought to have been light, instead it had remained dark. People could not understand why French and Spanish ships had been allowed to roam free. None could fathom where the enemy might land if not England. Lord Melville skulked under a cloud of fraud. When terrible news of Ulm arrived, Pitt had visibly slumped upon hearing it.[210] It felt like Britain stood alone on the edge of an abyss. A few days later the bitter-sweet news of Trafalgar reached home.

---

206 *The British Navy Triumphant*, 1805, 35.
207 Urban, *ibid*, 1160.
208 *Ibid*.
209 Johnson, 1813, 47.
210 *The Annual Register, ibid*, 218. It was a defeat that did not include British troops.

As the poet gazed out the window to the street below he happened to see a woman and a sailor walk by arm in arm, while on the other side lurked a group of ne'er-do-wells in the shadows. The contrast was startling and it gave him an idea. *Beauty faded and the world went dark, The sound of battle was loud and stark, Screams and groans rose as men lost their lives, To protect brothers and sisters, mothers and wives. Could the navy stand up to one man's tyranny? Could one British admiral fulfil his destiny? Would fate provide victory? Would they make a stand? With great guns blazing and swords in their hand?*

He re-read these first promising lines and smiled with pleasure. He instinctively knew he would suggest the battle had been a disaster for French and Spanish designs and that for Britain and her navy the heavy darkness had been broken by an unexpected dawn. It had been a revolution of fortune no one could have foreseen. Trafalgar showed the importance of Britain's senior service, and in stark tones the difference between French armies and the French navy. De Bourrienne would later write, 'This great battle afforded another proof of our naval inferiority.... . The battle of Trafalgar paralyzed our naval force, and banished all hope of any attempt against England.'[211] The sense of relief throughout Britain had been palpable. The Navy had delivered a drubbing to the enemy; people celebrated the battle and mourned the loss of a hero. The poet continued to write what would, he hoped, be his magnum opus. At dawn his wife awoke to find him still writing at the desk.

---

211 Bourrienne, 1832, 408.

Chapter 4

Britons Never will be Slaves

On taking over the deck the lieutenant solemnly went through the proper order of things. He took pains to note the ship's course, ensure the whole watch were up with lookouts relieved, ascertained the sails were properly trimmed and checked the backstays. He had to peer into the dimness for some time, eyes wide open, to make out uncertain shapes above. The courses were obvious but the topsails almost rumours. Eventually satisfied he turned his eyes inboard and caught sight of a midshipman.

'Mr Faulknor, with this freshening breeze we will shortly place hands at the relieving tackles.[212] Make sure you check the lower decks at every bell.'

'Aye, sir!' replied the taller, more sombre man.

A bashful gunner's mate, one of a dozen lascars onboard, stepped forward and knuckled his head.

'Ah, Indigo. Report the state of the guns every bell, if you please.' With a slight nod and grunt the sailor sauntered back into the shadows.

A few minutes later the new carpenter's mate arrived to report the level of water in the well.

The sounds and rhythm of the ship were a comfort to the lieutenant. He often wondered at man's ingenuity to build such things. A mere speck upon a wild sea but look how swiftly she flies![213] His only criticism was how she had been re-stowed. He considered the old girl rolled far too much in heavy seas and she was seldom dry; spray buffeted everyone on the weather deck and green water had been noted. But he loved the thought of a storm with plenty of sea room. Barbary lay a good ways off and there was no risk of a lee shore.

Soon enough both the master-at-arms and the carpenter appeared. The master-at-arms, a diffident fellow, reported that all fire and candles below had been extinguished and coppers secured. The carpenter, a man hard

---

212 Steel, P., 1804, 29. Relieving tackles were hooked to the tiller to aid the steering of a ship in heavy weather.

213 Similar to sentiments found in Rockwell, 1842, 2.

as nails, struck up a conversation. 'The stern-post, sir. Loose and terribly overworked she is. The third pintle of the rudder.[214] We shall have trouble with her soon enough and a heavy night ahead.'

When the master-at-arms and carpenter departed the lieutenant thought how some men like to worry one another at their pleasure.[215]

The sudden arrival of the captain gained his and the entire watch's attention. The old man's grizzled features and bluff manner were enough to send chills down the spine of anyone, even when partially hidden in the dark. He stomped over to his usual spot.

'It was providential we surveyed our stores today, yes?[216] But I note the watch bill needs attention. It looks old and dogged. See that it is changed.'

The lieutenant was used to the captain's curt manner. 'Yes, indeed sir. I will do so when relieved.'

'Hmm. With this wind there will be no divine service tomorrow.'

The captain placed a hand on the glass of the binnacle. He tried to rub away a smear but it didn't come off. 'Cloth!' he barked. The lieutenant, taken aback, was perplexed and mightily relieved when one was proffered him from out of the shadows. He quickly placed it beside the captain's hand.

'We should be more observant of dirty hands, yes?'

'Indeed, sir.'

'Indeed. You say that a lot, Mr Bartholey.'

The captain returned to his cabin, no doubt to stew over something or other. Probably whether to return the crew to two watches rather than the more indulgent three. Poor weather made it necessary and they would soon be close to the enemy. With sickness they were now short of hands, the more able idlers working the mainsail.[217] He saw one of them by the main-chains[218] scratching his behind.

The captain pretended to be a man of literature and breeding but was as coarse as a carding comb. He seldom praised anyone, was always disappointed with his officers, and liked to make men servile. But the lieutenant knew how to accommodate such a spiteful dotard – smile, truckle and flatter his vanity. He thought of other men more worthy of esteem. His

---

214 Similar to an account in Charnock, 1797, 9.

215 Said by the Earl of Pembroke in Act I Scene I of the play *Lady Jane Gray* by Rowe. See Bell, 1780, 15.

216 Article XXV of *Regulations Relating to His Majesty's Service at Sea*, 1787, 27. They were updated in 1808.

217 Steel's *Observations and instructions for the use of the Commissioned, the Junior, and other officers of the Royal Navy*, 1804, 64.

218 A platform to the side of a ship.

father for one, who had not only gained his manumission but had set up as a drayman in Kingston; and John Perkins who commanded the *Drake* and *Arab* with éclat. His example had been the reason he had joined the sea service.

The sea service. Apart from the recent fuss over Denmark, when it was deemed possible the Danish fleet might be seized by the French, almost everyone in the navy now suffered tedious and continual blockade. It had become the rule rather than the exception. Fatigue caused headaches, quarrels and outright rancour. There was no privacy, no variety, no alteration from routine.[219] Salt fare was a torture and sailors were no better off than monks cloistered in a damp cell. Their wives and sweethearts were distant memories and those poor women must have considered their men almost as gaol-birds. The ship smelled like a prison and the sick-list grew every day. If there had ever been an opportunity at least half the crew would have jumped ship. He thought back to the death of Pitt in 1806 when peace seemed possible, but such hopes had been ill-placed. They remained on perpetual blockade with no possibility of a decent prize.

There were sailors on British ships whose skin was not white. In December 1759 the *Litchfield* ran aground off the Barbary coast. A passenger wrote a letter: 'Our ship was about 900 tons burthen, manned with a hundred lascars, or black sailors.'[220] In 1806 Alderman Prinsep told Parliament that the East India Company was a nursery of British seamen and asked, 'by whom are the Company's ships now manned, and likely to be both in peace and war, while our enemy was attempting to rival us on the seas: By foreigners mostly when outward bound, and back principally by Lascars, natives or subjects of British India.... It was not interest, but necessity that ever induced the employ of black sailors on board the merchant ships... the British lascar ought in policy to be preferred to Danish or American sailors.'[221] As part of his lectures on yellow fever in 1806 and 1807 Edward Bancroft recounted how a French ship, the *Prevoyante* on passage to Halifax, buried two men, 'one French seaman, on the 25th of May, - and one black seaman, on the 26th'.[222] In 1826 it was written in a book of missionary tales how a ship struck rocks in the West Indies where, 'Soon after... the

---

219 Similar to the boredom expressed in Hannay, 1886, 140/141.
220 Wilkinson, 1764, 38. It appears the wreck was in the Red Sea. The author was Captain Barton.
221 *The Parliamentary Debates for 1806*, 1812, 1215.
222 Bancroft, 1821, 497.

boat washed overboard, with George Lambert, a free black seaman in it.'[223] Much later, in 1866, Commander Dawson related how he had served more than fifty years in the merchant marine and Royal Navy and that 'In the first year on the coast of Africa the whole of the crew, including the black men, were attacked by scurvy.'[224]

John Perkins, the Royal Navy's first ever black [mulatto] captain, often known as Jack Punch, was written about in *The Naval Chronicle*[225] on the occasion of his death in 1812. During the previous American War, 'he annoyed the enemy more than any other officer... [with] the immense number of prizes he took.' He commanded the *Punch* (10) and the brig-sloop *Drake* (14). Just before the war against revolutionary France he had been liberated from capture on Saint-Domingue. He was incarcerated in Jérémie for 'having supplied the people of colour with arms'.[226] Captain Nowell of the *Ferret* (12) stood in to the port with a note for his release but was refused. Joined by the *Diana* (32) Nowell went ashore, was surrounded by a mob, but gave an hour for local authorities to release their prisoner; which was complied with. When promoted post-captain in 1803, Perkins took command of the *Arab* (22). His life and conduct was inspirational to all naval officers.

As the Navy continued to expand, with the concurrent stresses of manning both a merchant marine and armies for overseas campaign, more and more foreign seamen had to be employed and by so doing the predominant white tone of fleets became less and less pronounced. Every ship needed seamen to pull ropes, man the guns and handle sails, and a man or woman's colour had no bearing upon their abilities. Thus manned, the Royal Navy was able to fulfil the aims of the British government and the admiralty.

After Trafalgar, blockade was the policy of both major naval combatants. The peace of Amiens made Bonaparte popular with the French, but as the treaty collapsed he realized that to beat Britain he had no choice but to reintroduce the unpopular *guerre de course*. French troops invested Hanover,[227] despite 'infringing the neutrality of Germany', and marched to Otranto to create two 'flanks'[228] to squeeze British commerce. On 20 June

---

223 Smith and Choules, 1832, 8.
224 *Journals of the Society of Arts*, 1866, 131.
225 *Vol XXVII*, 1812, 351/2.
226 Southey, 1827, 56. Details of Perkins's release from this source.
227 On 26 May 1803.
228 According to Mahan, 1902, 109. Otranto is in southern Italy.

1803 he issued a decree, as part of his plan to invade England, to bar British shipping all the way from the Elbe river to Brest.

Eventually Britain responded with her own Order of Blockade, 'imposed by Mr. Fox, and which was at that time loudly complained of both by France and America.'[229] It mirrored the French blockade. The French returned in kind with the Berlin Decree of 21 November 1806 that introduced the famous Continental System. This considered 'the British Islands to be in a state of blockade, and ordered all Englishmen in countries occupied by the French to be seized as prisoners of war.'[230] The French argued that Britain 'violated the law of nations, so far as regarded neutral vessels… [with] no other object but to obstruct the communications of other people, and elevate the industry and commerce of England upon the ruins of that of the Continent.'[231]

The continental system had to be conducted with real vigour so an 'army of locusts'[232] was unleashed to impose it. In a manuscript supposedly 'transmitted from St Helena in 1817'[233] an unknown author, possibly Bonaparte, argued that Britain would have continued to wage war as long as she had the 'wherewith to pay its expenses', so a war to ruin her credit had to be conducted. The continental system, this author argued, was both a 'banner and palladium' of French ideals and a spur to create a French manufacturing interest but it ultimately failed because it raised prices which was 'favourable to commerce' and it did not prevent a 'contraband trade'.

On 7 January 1807 Britain implemented an Order in Council regarding the seizure of neutral vessels trading with France and her allies, followed on 11 November 1807 with another Order that prohibited direct trade into Europe from any port or country, including the United States, from which the United Kingdom 'was excluded'.[234] America could trade directly with Sweden but all other goods had to be landed in England. It was stipulated that 'all ships proceeding thither should be captured, unless they had touched a British port, and paid a duty'. It was understood that the Royal Navy, the senior service, would be the means to this end.

It was tit-for-tat and France responded with the Decree of Milan which stated all ships that touched a British port were considered 'de-nationalized,

---

229 It was dated 16 May 1806. *Cobbett's Parliamentary Debates*, 1812, 779.
230 Dalgleish, 1892, 160.
231 Alison, 1847, 152.
232 Alison, *ibid*, 154.
233 *Manuscript Transmitted from St. Helena By An Unknown Channel*, 1817, 78-80.
234 *General Index to British and Foreign State Papers*, 1865, 327.

and a lawful prize, and further, that every vessel, to whatever nation she might belong, fitted out or going to England, or the British Colonies, or any country occupied by British troops, should be captured and confiscated.'[235]

Some observers considered these actions to go against international law. One problem was that to be 'respected' a blockade had to be conducted in force. According to William James, 'From the battle of Trafalgar to the peace of 1815, three-fourths of the British navy, at sea, were constantly employed in blockading the fleets of their enemies. Of the remainder, such as escaped the dull business of convoying, cruised about; but the only hostile ships that in general crossed their tracks, were disguised neutrals; from whom no hard knocks could be expected.'[236] But, whereas British fleets and squadrons were in the ascendant, with three-fourths of their number on blockade duty, 'There never was an adequate force stationed to effect a legal blockade of a third part of the coast included within the proclamation.'[237] Nevertheless the suppression of neutral trade and navigation did take place.

Even for Britain, the nation that then controlled the seas, her trade suffered for a number of years. In 1805 she boasted a merchant marine of 21,961 registered ships with 157,712 men and boys in employ,[238] but her imports declined from £53,600,000 in 1805 to £45,700,000 in 1808. Her exports managed to remain constant, around £50,000,000 per year from 1805 to 1808, and even climbed to £66,000,000 in 1809. The vast majority of her exports were shipped to Europe as 'notwithstanding all the evils of war, our mercantile navy [remained] on the increase... . In 1810 it was 164,195 [men and boys].'[239]

The purpose of blockade was to inflict 'severe distress on such of the enemy's subjects as were exposed to these measures of annoyance'.[240] For instance, the 1806 blockade of Venice shut off all sea traffic to the city so that inhabitants lacked fuel during the winter. A blockade could affect a whole nation. A proclamation by Sir Charles Cotton,[241] dated 28 April 1808 onboard the *Hibernia* (110) off Lisbon, talked of 'scarcity of grain'

---

235 Deane, 1870, 21.

236 James, 1817, 92/93.

237 Carey, 1815, 125.

238 *The Monthly Review*, 1814, pages 175 and 176. Following figures from this source. Imports climbed to more than £59,000,000 in 1809.

239 *The Monthly Review*, ibid.

240 *The Scots Magazine*, 1810, 452. The Venice blockade mentioned in *The Literary Panorama*, 1807, 200.

241 *Papers Presented to Parliament*, 1809, 245/246.

and 'other Articles of Necessity', and 'Calamities occasioned' through consequent famine. He argued how the blockade had been conducted in self-defence but he proposed an end to the distress caused throughout Portugal. It would have been similar elsewhere.

The distress caused by blockade had many question the ethics and conduct of the navy. In 1709 Barnaby Slush, in his *The Navy Royal, or a sea-cook turned projector,* wrote upon what he considered the terrible behaviour of sea officers towards their men. He believed that 'The Virtue, Equity, Sobriety, Generosity, and Gallantry of a Commander' affected the behaviour of sailors. He never used the word 'ethical' but he did use 'moral accomplishments' and 'moral certainty'.[242] He lived in a different age, but nearly a hundred years later the debate on morals in the navy was still ongoing.

In 1799 Alexander Duncan wrote strident essays on moral, political and divine matters with respect to the British navy. With inflated titles such as, *The several most resplendent naval victories during the currency of this just and necessary war, acquired by British valour, conduct, and courage, ought to be considered as most incontrovertible proofs of Divine favour to Great Britain*[243] he argued that 'whenever the navy and army lose the sense of all religious and moral obligation, which I trust, in God, they never will; from that moment you may date the decline, and foretell, without the spirit of prophecy, the final destruction and downfall of our monarchy, and the ruin of our happy constitution, both in church and state'.[244]

The *Literary Panorama* of 1807 included an extract from *The Naval Chronicle* for June of the same year in a piece titled 'Improved Moral Habits of British Seamen'. The article stressed how the allotment of pay to support families, better food and discipline and improved conditions on warships (which would have included the attitudes of officers towards their men) had been 'favourable to morals... . Venerate thyself, is a good moral precept, judiciously understood and practiced.' The extract included in this article stated, 'There is now a greater degree of decency of manners introduced into the messes, dress, and conduct of a seamen than formerly.'[245]

Around this time William Falconer reckoned that 'both the naval and military service have, by proper regulations and better instruction, been

242 Slush, 1709, 6, 44 and 94.
243 Duncan, 1799, 1.
244 *Ibid*, 34.
245 1808, 961. The article in *The Naval Chronicle* was titled 'Present Management and Discipline of the Navy Letter V' and appeared on pages 460-3, signed A.F.Y.

greatly elevated in the moral character within the last century.'[246] *Regulations Relating to His Majesty's Service at Sea* ensured punishments were handed out for anyone 'heard to Swear, Curse, or Blaspheme the Name of God'.[247]

However, a book published in 1821 bemoaned the lax morals of warships' men while in port, where 'It has become an established practice… to admit, and even invite, on board our ships of war, immediately on their arrival in port, as many prostitutes as the men, and, in many cases, the officers may choose to entertain, to the number, in the larger ships, of several hundred at a time; all of whom remain on board, domesticated with the company, men and boys, until they again put to sea.'[248] As a consequence there were scenes of 'riot and disorder' with 'obscenity, drunkenness, lewdness, and debauchery'. Wives and families who came onboard had to share the same decks with wanton women with no privacy, while the 'young men' were ever prey to their lures. Alcohol was regularly smuggled onto ships which made them places ill fit for people of polite society. A squadron would have swept a place like Dock and Plymouth clean of 'women of the town'.

Moral behaviour was often linked with religious observance, or seen through a lens of faith. Which is not to say religion was followed to any great depth on all warships. One lieutenant wrote in 1800, 'some Religious Tracts found their way on board the Fortitude, and shortly after that, I observed one of the Marines collect a number of his comrades into the guard-room, and read the Bible to them.'[249]

Edward Pellew, who commanded the *Nymphe* (36) at the start of the war against revolutionary France, was a highly religious man. In later life he stated that when 'he first entered the royal navy, a severity of discipline, and a coarseness of language and deportment prevailed among sea-officers, even of the highest rank, which is now almost… banished from the profession.'[250] Virtues of justice, fortitude, prudence and temperance had by then become more pronounced. Years of war, threats of invasion, distress of poverty, loss of life and actions of church, theatre and press[251] had had an effect.

---

246 Falconer, 1803, xxix.
247 Article III under *Rules of Discipline and good Government to be observed on Board His Majesty's Ships of War.*
248 *Statement Respecting The Prevalence of Certain Immoral Practices in His Majesty's Navy*, 1821, 1.
249 *Proceedings of the First Twenty Years of the Religious Tract Society*, 1820, 43.
250 Written about in 1833. He first went to sea, aged thirteen, in 1770 aboard the *Juno. The Sailor's Magazine and Naval Journal*, 1832, 372.
251 'Church, theatre and pressed' used by Captain Herbert in discussions in Parliament. *The Annual Register*, 1809, 114.

For many people of this era their beliefs and consciences led them to a disgust of the slave trade. Their Golden Rule was *do unto others as you would have others do unto you*. Although 'the English constitution [gave] freedom to every slave who may touch the British shores,'[252] in 1807 James Stephen reckoned that 'The number of Slaves carried from Africa in 1804, in ships cleared out from Great Britain, supposing their cargoes to have equalled, and not exceeded, the numbers limited by law, was 36,899... . This account, however, comprises the Slave ships *trading under British colours* only. If the British Slave Trade, carried on under American and Dutch colours [is included]... the dreadful amount of the human victims immolated at the shrine of our national avarice, would be greatly enlarged.'[253]

In 1807 a man who considered abolition and the role of Royal Navy to be inseparable, commenced a journal to discuss his personal hopes that the slave trade would one day end. *The navy, my dears, must be the means by which we restrict this terrible trade.* He lived in the rotten borough of Plympton Erle, where part of local society exhibited 'darling' attributes. He was considered well-meaning enough, but his companion, 'Lady Hamilton', was a menace. As the abolitionist stalked the roads and byways of the district his yapping and spiteful dog needed to be avoided for she bit more than her fair share.

A young couple who this abolitionist happened to meet conversed eagerly with him about Copenhagen, which was the news about town at the time. 'On the 19th of July, in consequence of the treaty of Tilsit, a demand was made by Great Britain for the surrender of the Danish fleet, which was required to be delivered up and to be carried to England, under a solemn promise of its restoration at the conclusion of a general peace.'[254] The Tilsit treaty was made between France and Russia, so Britain moved quickly to deter either of them from gaining Danish warships. She sent a fleet under Admiral Gambier comprised of the *Prince of Wales* (98); the *Pompee* (80); the 74s *Alfred, Brunswick, Captain, Centaur, Ganges, Goliath, Hercule, Maida, Orion, Resolution, Spencer* and *Vanguard*; the 64s *Dictator, Ruby* and *Nassau*; twenty-one frigates; various sloops, bombs and hundreds of transports. They sailed from Yarmouth on 26 July 1807 and 27,000 troops, mostly German, were landed on Danish soil before the ships sailed on to Copenhagen. They arrived in front of that city on 17 August 1807. The island of Zealand was surrounded and on

---

252 'Piomingo', 1810, 119.
253 Stephen, 1807, 27.
254 Allen, 1852, 202.

7 September 1807 the Danish capital was taken. Seventeen Danish ships of the line, two 32s and some smaller vessels were towed out and put to sea, and although old were set to join the British navy.[255] *More of a loss to Denmark than a gain to ourselves.*

The young couple went on to ask him why he had such an interest in abolition. He told them it stemmed from a 1778 visit to the Royal Academy. *Imagine, dear friends, a young man of tender heart on the verge of such an awakening.* There had been a painting on display that depicted Plymouth-born Brook Watson in the waters of Havana harbour with a boat full of sailors trying to save him from a shark. *That watery beast took away the poor man's lower right leg! A terrible ordeal – oh, worry not madam my dog is only playing with you – I was gratified to see the painting included a black sailor.*[256] *It opened my eyes so very much. As to Watson, well I think it cruel what Smollett later wrote about him – 'Watson, hapless elf! Shark-bitten once, but now a shark himself.'*[257] *Do you know the painting, my dears? It caused such a sensation at the time and it convinced me of the need to end this awful trade of slavery – Oh, Lady Hamilton!, please leave the nice woman's ankle alone.*

For the abolitionist recent years had been both a torment and a delight. In 1802 France reinstated slavery. He had felt outrage at the time but what could he do? Britain maintained the same trade. It was then that he decided to openly promote 'the movement' and spread the word.

He made it his business to get out and about and confront as many people as possible. His efforts resulted in many memorable 'little talks'. Such as one with a naval lieutenant and his wife held under the arches of the local grammar school. The abolitionist deftly managed to get them on to the topic of Thomas Clarkson's *An Essay On The Impolicy of The African Slave Trade.*[258] His dog had been cowed into silence after the man in blue had secretly given her a kick. The abolitionist asked, 'Is it true, my dear lieutenant, that advocates of the slave trade contend it is a nursery for our seamen? That it is highly dangerous to suppress such trade, as our seamen are a pillar of the state? Do you agree?'

The lieutenant did not agree, stating, 'It is a drain, and when I myself came across a slaver – you would not fathom the smell, sir – we tried to

---

255 Craik and MacFarlane 1849, 287. A result of the battle was that Russia turned against Britain until 1812.
256 John Singleton Copley's *Watson and the Shark.*
257 Smollett, 1794, 320.
258 Clarkson, 1788, 35.

press a few hands out of her but found none worth taking. I have seen much of slavery abroad and can state categorically that we tars do not care for it.'[259]

They talked of men involved in the trade, who did not have to 'stand upon character'. 'Not like the navy!' opined the abolitionist. 'Your fine service would never countenance such men, I am sure. You need true hearts to be successful in battle!'

The lieutenant confirmed it was difficult to recruit sailors for slave ships in ports where it was 'carried on' for most knew what was involved. 'Yet, often when seamen are paid off from their employment – for instance when the Greenland trade returns to refit – they have to join a slave ship for the pay. And there are lures to catch the unwary. A sailor might be promised to be made a mate, but disrated on some charge or other when at sea; or they might be made blind drunk by a landlord and charged with a bill they cannot afford. Threatened with either jail or employment on a slave-vessel they normally opt for the latter.'

The abolitionist nodded in shocked understanding. 'Oh, I see. I believe Clarkson admits the reason he dislikes the slave trade is "because the cruel treatment of seamen in this trade is notorious"? Is that true? It is! Oh, how can Englishmen tolerate it?'

Another 'talk' took place on the slopes of the ruined Norman castle where Lady Hamilton bit a child's hand. Ignoring the stifled howls the abolitionist had turned to a group of laughing labourers close by. 'I have it on good authority, friends, that on Jamaica the naval yard has many slaves,[260] but I am sure you would find work there.'

After the rough men had rudely walked off he harrumphed and turned back to the mother who fussed over her child. 'I have it on good authority, ma'am, that a recent petition by a Mr Lyon, agent for Jamaica, has been reported to Parliament where he argues that "the cultivation of the island... cannot be carried on without supplies of African negroes".[261] For shame, we should send some of our lazy labourers there so that no man would suffer bondage. I see your little girl is over-tired, for she cries so much.'

---

259 William Wilberforce reckoned, 'The fact was, that of 12,263 seamen employed in the African trade, 2,643 died in one year, whereas only 323 died out of the same number employed in the West India trade.' See Urban, 1804, 282.

260 The county was Surrey, see the *Annual Register* for 1793 (printed in 1797), 422. This county, which included Kingston, had 16,659 slaves out of a total population of 26,478. There was reported a total population on the island of 291,400 with 250,000 'Negro slaves'.

261 *Cobbett's Parliamentary Debates*, 1807, 833.

While he walked close to the park of Saltram[262] he managed to waylay two old women wrapped up in winter clothing and bore them senseless with extracts from a magazine he happened to have with him. It 'touched on the improvement which would take place in the colonial system, by the abolition of the Slave Trade; as the greatest drain upon the British army was the thousands of soldiers annually sent to protect the Whites in the West Indies against the slaves.'[263] He stood with his hands behind his back and pronounced like a lord in parliament, 'My dear ladies, we must include the Royal Navy and the Royal Marines in that equation. Do you know that slaves work the Jamaica naval yard? The First Report of the Commissioners – remember they had looked so deeply into affairs here at Plymouth? – considered abuses of a Mr Smith and Mr Dick and found them to have used "several of their own slaves as artificers and labourers, for whose service they received the pay of government".[264] For shame! Oh dear... it appears Lady Hamilton has taken a dislike to your shawl, madam. Hmm, she normally ignores such cheap material.'

For all his bumbling and affronts the abolitionist was often invited to local soirées and dinners, so long as he was without his dog. He wore all the latest fashions, was enchanted with the attention, and drank far too much. The slave trade was not the only topic of interest as dinner talk often happened upon naval things. He knew next to nothing about a warship – at best he was a fresh-water sailor – but he listened and soaked up much. At one dinner it was mentioned how the French navy had suffered recently. He could not resist interjecting to tell a story he knew of events in the Indian Ocean. 'Admiral Linois, if you recall, was a rum fellow. His ship the *Marengo* had with her an accompaniment of three frigates and a brig and he tried to harry a British merchant fleet. What a devil, but what a jig our excellent Captain Dance taught him! That Frenchman learned a new quadrille then.'

A sour old man present gave him a cold stare: 'Do you make a pun, sir? What piffle.'

But the abolitionist was proud, and not bright enough to know when to stop. 'I assure you, sir, that the dance made was most splendid. Imagine, our warships and merchantmen against such an enemy fleet. The very boldness shown by our sailors and lascars to confront the French and deal them a blow. And a blow they did give. There was no indecision, only stout British courage. Those French fellows turned and fled! What did he save us? Eight millions,

---

262 The largest mansion in the county. Britton and Brayley, 1803, 143.
263 *The European Magazine*, 1806, 65.
264 *Cobbett's Parliamentary Debates*, 1805, 883.

I am told. He showed us what the French navy is all about, and how our own black fellow men are worthy of praise. Dance's demonstration decidedly deserved decoration! I raise a toast to all sailors and lascars!' His alliteration impressed some diners but not the old man who thereafter ignored him.

The dinner continued and by the end of the evening the abolitionist regaled everyone, his nose bright red, upon how one day slavery would surely end. 'For of what has Wilberforce reminded us? "That there is neither Greek nor Jew, circumcision nor uncircumcision, Barbarian, Scythian, bond nor free: but Christ all, and in all."[265] Yes, and Parliament – praise be Lord Grenville! – has finally hazarded an innovation to bring about *An Act for the Abolition of the Slave Trade*. What delight! I knew this day would come. After the first of January 1808 there will be no more trade conducted out of Africa. Not by ourselves anyway. Such a positive and humane step, don't you think? I suppose it will fall to our navy, and men like Dance, to see that this is complied with.'

Which was the case, for the senior service was the means by which Britain could impose her will. For 1807 there was voted 130,000 men for the sea service[266] and a very small West Africa (or Preventative) squadron brought together to blockade the entire west African coastline. It was a time when the French were not as diminished in strength as the British public knew or liked to admit[267] so the remit of only two warships, *Solebay* (32) and *Derwent* (18), was given to patrol the African coast roughly from the river Gambia in the north to Little Fish Bay in the south. It was an excessively large area to cover.

Sierra Leone, a colony originally set up for 'philanthropic' reasons but then in severe decline, was transferred to the British government and made a safe haven with 'all captured slaves, rescued from slave ships by the English cruisers... brought into Sierra Leone, as their asylum'.[268] This part of the coast happened to be well known for Kroomen, black merchants and seamen were often used by British merchant ships that required hands.[269] By the 1840s British warships who worked this station had them as part of their complements.

Sir James Lucas Yeo, who knew the station well, later wrote a letter in which he said, 'Though fewer negroes have been enslaved since the

---

265 Wilberforce, 1807, front cover.
266 *Naval Chronicle*, 1807, 172.
267 See James, 1824, 8 to 11.
268 Newcomb, 1860, 77.
269 *The Edinburgh Review*, 1812, 69.

abolition acts took place, with respect to this country, yet the cruelty to those taken away by the Spaniards and Portuguese, has increased quadruple; and those acts appear to have had no other effect, than of transferring the Slave Trade to Spain and Portugal.'[270] He illustrated this with an account of a Portuguese vessel of 120 tons found with more than 600 slaves onboard in a 'horrid state'.[271]

The issue of Portugal and the Brazils came up in Parliament. Lord Grenville observed on 25 February 1808 that with the act to end slavery ministers should have refused commercial treaties with Portugal, unless that nation likewise abolished slavery, for 'The Brazils must exist as an independent state, by the protection afforded by the British navy.'[272] Britain therefore ended her involvement in the slave trade, used her navy to patrol western Africa, all the while protecting the Brazils which imported slaves from Portugal.

On 14 May 1811 Britain took further steps with the *Slave Trade Felony Act* that punished anyone involved in slavery with fourteen years transportation and hard labour.[273] But after war against the United States broke out in 1812 patrols against slave ships had to be abandoned. Only after 1815 was the squadron reinstated. Slavery was made 'piratical' by the British government in 1824, but it took decades to fully destroy the trade.

One cold and rainy day back in 1810, all these things lay in the future as the abolitionist visited his favorite draper in Plymouth. Standing outside the small shop he got into a difficult to and fro with a curt Cornishman. The Plympton man considered the visitor from across the Tamar more foreign than the French, so when he stated that the act to end slavery would destroy British commerce the abolitionist became cantankerous. He put his hands behind his back and jutted out his jaw. 'What do you mean, sir? Explain yourself!'

The Cornishman waved his cane around like a baton: 'Our commerce, sir, will surely suffer. The French think so. They say we "shop-keepers" will be undone by our morality.'

The abolitionist knew exactly what the man referred to. The *Annual Register* had stated that abolition 'threatened ruin to the most valuable branch of British commerce, and proved to the world, that this "nation of shopkeepers," as it had been sneeringly styled by the French, was susceptible

---

270 Marryat, 1818, 93.

271 *Ibid.*

272 *Cobbett's Parliamentary Debates,* 1808, 734.

273 Eardley-Wilmot, 1860, 8.

of the finest feelings, and might be induced to pay homage to the purest principles of morality.'[274] He felt affronted for he considered Britain a land of liberalism, where reason and moral values held a hand upon the tiller of state and acted as lights in the darkness. So he in turn thrust out his chin and replied, 'Our principles are important, sir. Slavery has no place in a civilised world. It is an aberration. We are prepared to defend our principles, sir. Do you know that there is a bounty per head for all slaves liberated? A British warship can earn 40*l*[275] for each man, 30*l* for each woman and 10*l* for every child released from capture. We reward 'principled' fellows for doing their moral duty, sir![276] It is our principles that make Britons united and great!'

He stomped off, annoyed he had failed to impress his adversary but more so that Lady Hamilton had not worried the other man's leg. He would have liked to see him wince in pain.

The local heat of abolition had by then somewhat abated as bedraggled troops defeated at Corunna returned in dire condition. Their tents were suddenly arrayed on the Hoe, highly visible, and typhus raged amongst them.[277] The effects of war, so often hidden from home shores, had settled heavily amongst civilians. It was all they could think about, and the war still had to be won.

---

274 *The Annual Register,* 1809, 110.

275 Pound, as in *lsd – libra pondo*; this sign was used into the mid-nineteenth century.

276 *The Monthly Anthology Vol X*, 1811, 277.

277 Up until 27 March 1809 Plymouth harboured 2432 sick troops. Creighton, 1894, 166.

Chapter 5

And Every Shore it Circles Thine

The chaplain had hurt his humerus, but he did not think it funny. Neither how all of the men, bar himself and two others, had been lost. The once raucous crew, the *forma informans*[278] of the ship, were no more. They had given life to the watches, to the guns, to everything upon two wooden decks; they had struck terror into the enemy and for years had baffled the sea and wind in all its fury. When in final peril for their lives their hearts had never faltered but at the bitter end it was every man for himself and all for God.[279] Their earned experience and knowledge could not deflect the final reckoning. It was not an enemy fleet that killed them but the wind, the sea, and a rocky shore. *And behold, there arose a great storm on the sea, so that the boat was being covered with the waves.*[280]

For five days now they have stumbled over rough and rocky ground with only brackish water to drink and the rancid meat of one small lizard that had given them violent cholic and retching. They had to shelter during the unbearable heat of the day and walk only in the cool hours of the morning and evening.

In normal times the chaplain's shrunken cheeks make him resemble Aeolus the God of the Winds about to blow a gale, but with a 'cain-coloured beard'[281] and wild unkempt hair he looks more the lunatic. The other two look even worse.

As another night arrives they find a large round rock to settle on. Their stomachs rumble and they are soon tormented by flies. The mute instantly falls asleep. When all is silent the Scotsman says, 'Twas Auld Clootie that brought us ill.'

The chaplain thinks awhile. 'The Devil, you mean? Is that why you carry some coral?'

---

278 The force that animates. The run of thought that follows mirrors Slush, 1709, 2.
279 Slush, *ibid*, 12.
280 Matthew 8:24.
281 Yellow, from Shakespeare's *Merry Wives of Windsor* I. IV. Simple says, 'No, forsooth: he hath a little wee face, with a little yellow beard; a Cain-coloured beard.'

'Aye. If I'd have had it afore the storm we would ne'er have run up the beach. I saw tha' light in the trees and a-wished I had some then.'

The chaplain thought back to the day before the storm when the starboard watch wailed out as a ball of light appeared in the crosstrees. Superstitious to a fault they thought it to be corpus sancti.[282] It was a rare and wondrous display of nature, God's glory made manifest. *Even the winds and the sea obey him.*

But the lord sent a great wind into the sea, and there was a mighty tempest, so that the ship was like to be broken.[283]

The storm came, waves reared up like mountains and broke in *strange* and dangerous ways. The chaplain felt that this tempest was no punishment but God's will. *Then the mariners were afraid.* One seaman was lost from the main topsail yardarm before they could lower the top-sails and after that he noticed the crew cursed less and adopted a more sombre mood. When the hurricane hit in all its fury they were at risk of being pooped. The ship had difficulties steering. In his cabin, to the muffled sound of the pumps, he had consulted his book of common prayer: *O Eternal Lord God, who alone spreadeth out the heavens, and ruleth the raging of the sea.*[284]

He had fallen asleep but was awoken by the sound of a great tumult and his cabin leaking water. On deck he heard lookouts shouting 'breakers ahead!' No seaman himself, he got in the way, and was pushed and buffeted and called a mealy-mouthed lubber. When the ship struck rocks he was thrown to the deck where he cracked his head and bit his tongue. Three huge swells turned the ship, floated it some distance and caused her to strike more rocks. He had lain amid a boiling foam with great surges of water which pushed him so that he collided with a loose gun, one of the few not thrown overboard. With every wave the ship was forced to heel closer to the surf. One sailor, his face half dirt and half blood, managed to get the chaplain upright, and only then did he see a beach some distance off. Many men had already been thrown into the water where waves took them away. One had been the captain.

The rigging and sails fell and she broke up amid a great noise of wind, surf and wood made splinters. The chaplain was thrown into the sea and felt the sting of stone and coral under him. He must have passed out but came

---

282 St Elmo's fire. The biblical quote is from Matthew 8:27.

283 Jonah 1:4. The next quote is Jonah 1:5

284 Part of the morning and evening service for ships at sea. *The Book of Common Prayer*, 1743, 25.

to with a ringing in his ears while someone dragged him through the surf to the beach. He coughed up water and fainted again.

He awoke to a troublesome scene. He lay under a lone bush, the Scotsman and a mute his only living companions. The other two men had been so agitated by events they exhibited strange behaviour. Somehow the mute had a boatswain's call which he piped endlessly while capering around like Joseph Grimaldi, the clown of Sadler's Wells. The Scotsman rocked on his haunches and repeated words about him being captain of the mess and his mates *always well behaved, with two jackets, three shirts, waistcoat, three pair of trousers and two pair of shoes,*[285] only Tom Kettle the one cap having lost his hat overboard and none in slops.

Dead bodies were everywhere but nothing else. There was no wreck to stay with, not even a barrel. As soon as they had recovered their wits they reckoned their situation and decided the only way to survive was to walk all the way to Port Jackson. They were glad to leave the beach for by then it stank with decay. Days of pain, thirst and despair followed. They noted the sun each morning and made their way towards the north-east. With no map, compass, nor any arms they were at the mercy of a dangerous land.

They lay upon a rock, the only sound being the mute softly blowing his boatswain's call. The chaplain rubbed his elbow and considered the southern stars above. The moon was large and bright and upside down.[286] Either that or the world was. He thought to himself, how many wrecks have there been in this war? How many warships and men lost to the sea? His own brother had suffered two such misfortunes, one in Plymouth Sound and one off France – for *God moves in a mysterious way, His wonders to perform; He plants His footsteps in the sea, And rides upon the storm.*[287]

They are so far from home. So far from hope. *Yea, though I walk through the valley of the shadow of death, I will fear no evil, for you art with me.* And what was with him? Strangely, memories of music. Handel's Messiah. *Hallelujah!* Mozart's Lacrimosa. *Judicandus homo reus.*[288] Rule Britannia! *And every shore it circles thine.* Every shore, even an empty and desolate one such as this.

In the cool morning it was discovered the mute had died. Searching his remains they found a wicked wound on his leg, black and putrid. They decided to leave him, knowing wild dogs troubled the horizon but too weak

---

285 Steel, 1806, 51.
286 The moon appears to turn the further one moves from the northern hemisphere into the southern.
287 Words by William Cowper in 1774. Southey, 1849, 539.
288 The guilty man to be judged.

to bury the corpse. The chaplain uttered a quiet prayer, then followed the Scotsman into dry, flat, treeless terrain. By now neither of them cared about the other. It was all they could do to make the supreme effort of walking. The chaplain took comfort in remembering that the day will come when *there will be no more death nor mourning nor crying nor pain.*[289]

Port Jackson lay more than a thousand miles away.

The Navy suffered further wrecks after war returned. The *Augustus* gunboat ran aground on the Hoe in 1801, the *Crane* (14) on rocks west of the Hoe in 1806 and the *Amethyst* (38) against Cony Cliffs, Mount Batten, in 1811. On 16 January 1806 the *Hibernia* (110) lay at Cawsand from where she sent her launch round to Plymouth for stores. Manned by a 'lieutenant, a midshipman, and 43 seamen'[290] on her return she had to bear away, due to increased winds, and weather the Mewstone. This small triangular rock of 'bold outline' lies east of the sound[291] and from there the launch hoped to make the safety of the Yealm river. However, the launch got into difficulties between the Shag Stone and Renney Rocks. Her mast fell by the board, she struck and turned over. The lieutenant and twenty-three men made it ashore but the rest drowned. Only seventeen bodies were recovered. The *Naval Chronicle* reported one 'shipwreck of twenty-four persons who perished so near to shore... their cries could be distinctly heard'.[292]

The locations of naval wrecks between 1801 and 1815 show the dominance of the Royal Navy, a Neptune whose trident touched every shore. In 1801 the senior service maintained a permanent Channel fleet, Mediterranean fleet, North Sea fleet, squadrons for Ireland, India, the Leeward and Windward Islands, Jamaica and a host of guardships; all added to by squadrons despatched against the French, into the Baltic, off Cadiz, the Cape of Good Hope, North America and Newfoundland and amongst neutral islands. Naval theatres and operations sent warships far and wide so that in 1801 the *Forte* (50) sank in Jeddah's harbour in the Red Sea; in 1802 the *Sensible* (16) stranded south of Trincomalee; the *Porpoise* (12) sank off New South Wales in 1803[293]; the *Sheerness* (44) was lost in a hurricane off Trincomalee in 1805; in 1809 the *Agamemnon* (64) ran on shore in Maldonado Roads, Rio de la Plata; *Diana* (10) sank off Rodrigue

---

289 Revelation 21:4.
290 *The Annual Register*, 1806, 8. Further details from this source.
291 Page, 1895, 283.
292 *Naval Chronicle*, 1799, 428.
293 Now Queensland.

in the East Indies in 1810; in 1812 the *Centinel* (12) ran ashore near Rügen in the Baltic; and the *Daedalus* (38) sank off Ceylon in 1813.[294]

As well as storms, submerged rocks, shoals and islands were part of the many perils of the sea, and sailors long argued that something should be done to lessen the risks of navigation. The Admiralty created the Hydrographic Department in 1795 when newly appointed hydrographer of the navy Alexander Dalrymple took the reins, until dismissed for 'excessive zeal' in 1808 when Captain Thomas Hannaford Hurd took up tenure. Dalrymple wrote what was considered the first hydrographical work, *An Essay On The Most Commodious Modes of Marine Surveying*, in 1771. His task proved 'onerous and important, involving not only the collecting, collating, and publishing a large number of charts, but also the organising a department till then non-existent.'[295] When created, the department received observations from naval officers and masters engaged in navigation and exploration around the globe, yet it required five years to publish its first chart. Soon after Dalrymple left office he died and gifted many hydrographic and geographical books as part of a large library.[296]

The Hydrographic Department helped the senior service become a more scientific and effective force. Over time it propelled Britain to the forefront of hydrographic surveys, especially from 1828 under Rear Admiral Francis Beaufort, and the department advanced 'to the inestimable benefit of commerce, both British and foreign'.[297]As the years between 1801 and 1815 were mostly ones of war Britain had to put aside efforts to explore and survey coastlines but HMS *Investigator* was active from 1801 to 1803 (until considered unseaworthy and paid off at Plymouth in 1806). In her brief time she surveyed the southern coast of Australia: 'Recherche archipelago, the south of Australia, Nuyts archipelago, Waldegrave and Flinders' islands, Investigator group, Cape Catastrophe, and Port Lincoln were partly examined in turn... . Spencer gulf, Kangaroo island, Gulf of St. Vincent, and Encounter bay, working through Bass strait to Port Phillip.'[298]

The British were not alone in exploring and charting the world's coasts. Captains Baudin and Hamelin of France explored Australia with their ships *Naturaliste* and *Géographe* in 1801 and 1802. An account of the Russian navy's *Nadeshda* and *Neva*'s circumnavigation, made between

---

294 All wrecks mentioned in Gilly, 1857.
295 Stephen, 1888, 403.
296 Chambers, 1872, 429.
297 *The Popular Science Monthly*, 1876, 520.
298 Dawson, 1830, 22.

1803 and 1806, was published in 1813 in a two-volume work called *Voyage Around The World*. Both ships had been British. Whaling fleets and foreign merchants added much to the knowledge of the world's seas.

In late 1810 an invalid who lived in Torpoint, opposite Dock town across the river Tamar, bemoaned the then low state of British nautical exploration. He considered there was not enough! He secretly held hopes that one day he might patronise an expedition to discover some strange somewhere in the South Seas for there remained so much to discover. At the very least, he thought, the admiralty should send a ship on a voyage of discovery.

His house was modest. It had one small wing facing the naval yard at Dock, visible across the river, and when wheeled to a window he would gaze out for hours. He found the sight of ships lying in the Hamoaze most gratifying. His housekeeper knew of his knowledge of the sea but avoided talk of his terrible burns and lack of legs for the only time she had ventured to do so he had thrown a Toby jug in anger. She pitied him because he was obviously in pain and lonely. Fearing to venture out and upset young children he opted to remain indoors. What kept him active were his thoughts, books and periodicals on hydrographic and nautical themes, old instruments of navigation and an antique globe. He liked to turn the globe with his one remaining hand to find places he had sailed near, and wonder about the parts unknown. Northern Canada and most of Africa were vague but the Pacific was dotted with discovered islands. He had a fancy for the development of New South Wales and New Holland because, as his globe showed him, although they were on the opposite side of the world British influence reached that far. Botany Bay, the transportation of convicts and local wildlife kindled his interest. He longed to see a kangaroo. When he read in *The European Magazine* how 'The native of New Holland is found in the genuine state of nature'[299] he thought of Rousseau. What other gardens of paradise, he wondered, remained to be discovered? Dock town had been transformed in a short time, so he assumed Port Jackson and Sydney Cove might do the same. Convicts had been shipped there since 1787 so he thought these two ports to be thriving places and did not realise how they struggled with bouts of food scarcity.

He was delighted with a recent account written by John Savage, a surgeon, of his experiences in New Zealand and the Bay of Islands. When he read, 'the timber and flax produced here may at some future time be found highly valuable'[300] and fir 'grows here to an amazing height'.[301]

---

299 For 1804, page 128.
300 Savage, 1807, 8.
301 *Ibid.*

He became a polymath of naval ideas and events. He owned everything ever made public by Nevil Maskelyne, the Astronomer Royal, and boasted the most recent publications of *The Nautical Almanac and Astronomical Ephemeris,* and Michael Taylor's *Tables of Logarithmic Sines and Tangents to every Second of the Quadrant.* Pride of place on his shelves was given to Tobias Mayer's *Tables of the Sun and Moon;* Joseph Jérôme Lefrançois de la Lande's *Astronomy;* and Nathaniel Bowditch's *New American Practical Navigator,* a man reckoned to have 'corrected many thousand errors existing in the best European works of the kind; especially those in the Tables for determining the latitude by two altitudes, in those of difference of latitude and departure, of the sun's right ascension, of amplitudes, and many others necessary to the Navigator.'[302]

Old navigational instruments lay on a table and when the invalid considered them he smiled knowing that Schomberg had written, 'It is an object of amusement and utility for sea officers to be acquainted with the times of invention and introduction of the many mathematical instruments, charts, &c. by which we are enabled to traverse the immense ocean, in almost perfect security. The near approach of the discovery of the longitude in these modern days, by the ingenuity, industry, and astronomical abilities of Mr. Wichel's lunar observations, and Mr. Harrison's invention of the time-keeper, have proved truly beneficial to mariners.'[303] *Indeed they had!*

He liked to study azimuth compass-cards, old pilot books and domestic and foreign charts and maps. With sea charts he marvelled how they disagreed on one major point. British ones placed 'their first meridian at their royal observatory at Greenwich... the French at their observatory at Paris, while the other maritime nations... from the isle of Fer'.[304] What they did share in common was how they demarcated coasts, bays, rivers, shoals, rocks, banks and points of prevalent wind.[305]

His true mania was for safety. Anything that could improve the conditions and lives of sailors received his intense scrutiny; for instance, the voyage of *Lady Nelson* (6) in 1802 to conduct an experiment with sliding keels, designed to be screwed upwards into the vessel when needed to decrease the draft of water. Sliding keels were an 'ingenuity of Captain John Schank, of the Royal

---

302 Bowditch, 1807, 'report'.
303 *The Monthly Review*, 1803, 343. It was actually George Witchell and John Harrison.
304 Tuckey, 1815, 8 and 9. The Island of Fer, or El Hierro, is the southernmost island of the Canaries.
305 Moore, 1801, under CHA

Navy, formerly one of the Commissioners of the Transport Board'[306] who had first planned them in 1774. So long ago, he thought, but this long war had caused the naval administration to become more open to innovation. It turned out that *Lady Nelson* made a memorable voyage. When she first entered the Channel out of Gravesend, in January 1800, she rode out a storm in comfort while other ships were driven ashore. Afterwards she outsailed everything of a similar size, but in Portsmouth her carpenter and two other seamen had deserted her, not thinking the ship capable of a long voyage. They were proved wrong. From the Cape of Good Hope to Sydney Cove the captain, confident of his small vessel, sailed at a higher latitude than normal[307] and so *Lady Nelson* reached Port Jackson after seventy-one days passage and was the first naval ship to pass successfully through the Bass Strait.

It was therefore hoped that sliding keels would make ships 'sail faster, steer easier, and tack and wear quicker, and in less room. They would carry more, and draw less water... [and] ride more easy at anchor... [and] In case of shipwreck, of springing a leak, or of a fire, they are more safe, and more likely to be saved.'[308] *More safe!* The invalid thought this was where the future lay. Keep men alive to fight a war. He believed that more stable warships would gain an advantage over the enemy, make the landing of troops easier, and the senior service a more potent superpower. The wooden wall, the bulwark of the nation, would be made more formidable.

The invalid kept a list of almost everything reported in the papers or periodicals. He would have his housekeeper place a large ledger upon the table and either open it to a specific page for him to read or write in an entry of engagement or battle as dictated by himself. The first entry was of the *Doris* (36) who confronted the *Affronteur* (14) on the day of declaration in 1803, followed by the *Minotaur* (74) who had captured the *Franchise* (36) on 28 May 1803.[309] Thereafter it was a litany of similar actions, cutting outs and the occasional mishap. For instance, how the *Minerve* (38) ran aground off Cherbourg and had to withstand ten hours of bombardment from shore before she surrendered.[310]

He liked to read of the captains and officers involved in naval engagements, of their lives to date, and he held a private delight with some

---

306 *The European Magazine, ibid*, 41.
307 39 degrees South. Dawson, 1830, 36.
308 *The European Magazine, ibid*, 42.
309 Allen, 1852, 64. Other ship accounts from this source.
310 2 July 1803.

of their names: Jahleel Brenton, commodore Querangal, Barrington Dacres, Philip Dumaresq and Zachary Mudge to name but a few.

His ledger painted a picture of gallantry and enterprise: of commodore Hood's reduction of St Lucie, 21 June 1803, with the 74s *Centaur* and *Courageux* and smaller vessels, with the island of Tobago[311]; how Demerara, Essequibo and Berbice had been exchanged into British hands; of blockades against St Domingue ports and other West Indies islands; the lame exploits of French Rear Admiral Linois in the East Indies; Collingwood and events in the Dardanelles, at the Cape and South America; the siege of Danzig; the captures of Madeira and Curaçao; peace with Spain and war against Russia; the capture of Senegal and Martinique. All told wonderful and great adventures. Undistracted by outside influences he was able to perceive the full power and reach of the Navy. He found it both gratifying and frightening. What then must the enemy think?

By 1810 the Royal Navy was larger and stronger than ever before. She boasted 692 ships in commission with 72 ships for harbour service for a grand total of 1,048 ships and vessels.[312] In commission there were 5 first rates, 7 second rates, 96 third rates (for a total of 108 line ships); 7 fourth rates not classed as line ships and 2 two-decker fifth rates; 132 fifth rates; 23 sixth rates; 242 sloops; eight bombs; 78 gun-brigs and 73 cutters for a total of 664 active cruisers. The rest was made up of transports, stores-ships, a survey vessel and advice boats. Captures made during 1810 further added to the fleet: the 40s *Astrée, Bellone, Canonnière, Manche, Minerve* and *Vénus* (renamed *Nereide*); the 36s *Iphigénie* and *Néréide* (renamed *Madagascar*); and the *Nécessité* (28) were all taken.[313]

The invalid owned a recent copy of *Journals of the House of Commons* that laid out how there had been voted 145,000 seamen and marines with a total budget granted for the sea-service throughout the year of £19,822,000.10.0; and 'The TOTAL of the Ordinary Estimate of His Majesty's Navy, for the year 1810, amounts to ONE Million Five Hundred and Eight Thousand Four Hundred and Fifty-one POUNDS, Fifteen Shillings and Eleven Pence,'[314] a sum that only covered wages for Superannuated Sea Officers, the yards, pensions and allowances, ships and vessels in ordinary, victuals, repairs, half-pay, and bounties to chaplains. Under a separate list of pensions it stated that £900 had been authorised for John Marsh 'in consideration of

---

311 James, 1826, 299.
312 *Abstract of the Royal Navy Number 18,* 1821.
313 James, 1886, 115.
314 *Journals of the House of Commons,* 1810, 523.

his Services, as late one of the Commissioners for Victualling His Majesty's Navy', and £24 for Thomas Harley, 'late a Seaman on board the Valiant Transport, for the loss of both legs.'

The report laid out costs of forty-eight warships then building, eighteen warships ordered to be built and twenty-four being repaired at the King's Yards of Chatham, Deptford, Sheerness, Portsmouth, Plymouth and Woolwich; at Milford; and at merchant yards found at Bucklers Hard, Bursledon, Dartmouth, Fishbourn, Harwich, Liverpool, in the Medway, Northam, Paul, Ringmore, along the Thames, Sandgate, Topsham, Turnchapel and Warsash for a total cost of £1,309,574. Plymouth was building the *Union* (98) and the 38s *Nisus* and *Menelaus*; fitting out for sea the *Royal George* (110), *Barbette* (22), the 16s *Leucadia* and *Nearque*; and repairing the *Ocean* (98), *Malta* (84), the 74s *Dragon* and *Spencer*, the *Acasta* (40), the 38s *Didon* and *Immortalité*, the 16s *Electra*, *Peterell* and *Seagull* and the 14-gun brig *Insolent*. He could make out some of them from his window, with gangs of labourers all over them.

Sitting at his window he could also see, with the aid of a spyglass held up for him, the numerous and busy teams of dockyard workers 'blowing away the Rock and completing the Wall at the West front of the Ropehouses',[315] building a new boat pond and landing place with all the dirty work needed to lay pipes, repair and change water cocks, pumps and winches. His housekeeper, whose husband worked a boat to move materials up and down the river, told him of the work done to build a new pitch-house, painter's shop, hoophouse, hemp-house, white and black yarn houses and a storehouse. There was continual activity that required large public funds to sustain. And if that was not enough there were the costs of the Transport Office, stated at £3,936,750,[316] and ordnance.

With the continual need to repair and make up for losses there was constant worry over supplies of British oak. In 1810 the *Minotaur* (74); *Lively* (38); the 36s *Iphigenia*, *Magicienne*, *Nereide*, *Nymphe* and *Sirius*; the *Pallas* (32); the 16s *Fleche* and *Satellite*; the 12s *Conflict* and *Racer*; the 10s *Achate*, *Alban, Diana* and *Wildboar*; and the *Cuckoo* (4) were either wrecked, burned or captured.[317] Oak had become increasingly difficult to procure and was of high cost. In recent years Parliament had debated the possible use of teak to build warships.[318] In a debate of 25 November 1801

---

315 *Journals of the House of Commons, ibid*, 526.
316 *Ibid*.
317 All from James, 1886, 444/445.
318 Urban, 1801, 1200.

Sir William Pulteney reckoned teak superior to oak. Sir Francis Baring objected as, he said, teak would discourage the growing of British timber (he also wished to discourage the 'bringing over of Lascars'). Something had to be done and in 1803 the Admiralty ordered a 74- and a 36-gun warship to be built of teak at the East India Company's docks at Bombay. A further six 36- to 40-gun teak warships were ordered in 1804.[319] There already existed Indian-built ships transferred to the navy but these new ones were the first bespoke builds. Bombay was the obvious site to build them because 'The harbour is the best in India, and capable of containing any number of ships, to which it affords the most perfect shelter. Its docks admit ships of war of eighty guns: the yards are proportionately large, and well provided with marine stores of every description.'[320] Indian shipbuilders were also of high quality. A Mrs Graham went to India in 1809 and spent time in Bombay. In her journal she mentioned a visit to the yard and how she met the head of the dockyard, Jumsheedjee,[321] 'and was conducted by him all over the Minden, the first line of battle ship he ever built, with the pride of a parent exhibiting a favourite child. It was singular enough to see all the ship-wrights in white muslin dresses, caulking the ship with cotton instead of oakum.'[322] The *Minden* (74) was launched in 1810.

Of all ships launched in these years it was the *Caledonia* (120) that gripped the invalid's curiosity. That ship's keel had been laid down in the yard opposite him in 1805 and he eagerly watched her take shape. On the stocks her half constructed timbers reminded him of the bones of a horse's chest laid bare. Hundreds of timbers were brought together to make the ribs and sides. She was soon seen to be a monstrous 'castle of the seas' at 2,616 tons. Built to be the navy's most powerful warship, she had three decks of guns arranged along a length of 205 feet and a breadth of 53 feet 8 inches.[323] She could propel an awful amount of hot metal towards the enemy. From the waterline she towered above an observer. Such majesty, but what a sight! His housekeeper had been quite appalled by her.

His housekeeper. He considered her a kindly woman, but quite devious. One day he told her how he used to play the clarinet while at

---

319 Derrick, 1806, 222.

320 Smollett, 1801, 167

321 Also spelled in contemporary accounts as Jamsetji or Jamshedji. He was of the Wadia family.

322 *The Monthly Magazine*, 1815, 265.

323 *The Quarterly Review*, 1815, 450.

sea. It helped pass the time, he said, but it had been lost with the ship. To his surprise a clarinet arrived a few days later, with no note attached, which was quite similar to his old one. He quizzed her about it but she denied any knowledge. Touched by her kindness, he told her how seamen and officers have a fondness for music: 'We had a foretopman who played the fiddle,' he said, 'and another who hit the tambour like a demon. Both were very precious to the crew. They often played on the fo'c'sle, for jack likes to cut up a caper and sing a song whenever he can. Our captain encouraged it; he said it kept the men in equilibrium and out of the sick berth. We even shipped a dancing master once. I was told by a midshipman that a clarinet is far nobler than roaring a verse out of tune, or cursing at the world, so I devoted time to it. I often played Dibdin[324] as others sang the words.

> *But the standing toast that pleas'd the most*
> *Was - the wind that blows, the ship that goes,*
> *And the lass that loves a sailor!*

I was fairly proficient by the time…' But he preferred not to think of that time so changed the subject. 'Remember how they once paraded captured Spanish treasure to music?'

The housekeeper certainly did remember that and excitedly replied, 'Of course I do! A mild day at the end of October 1799 it were. I stood beside the dockyard wall and watched the whole thing. What a crowd! There was artillery and waggons – sixty or so if I remember right, lor what a sight – with marines and a band of fifes and drums playing *Rule, Britannia!* and *God Save The King.*[325] There was hardly any wind to ruffle the British flag over the Spanish one.'

The wind. A simple word could get his mind wandering. In naval war whatever the size of a ship everything was predicated upon the wind. The invalid had been becalmed more than once and had suffered the terror of a lee shore many times on his old ship.

His old ship. He tried not to think of her. At night he slept fitfully and did everything in his power to remain awake during the day, for if he ever nodded off his dreams haunted him. And they were always the same. As fire engulfed the ship buckets had been handed out in a line. Gun ports were

---

324 Dibdin wrote many patriotic and well regarded ballads. Dibdin, 1811.
325 *Naval Chronicle*, 1799, 544. The treasure was from the two Spanish 34s, *Thetis* and *Santa Brigida*.

opened to allow thick black smoke to pour out. There had been such heat it was impossible to remain below.

The ship's schoolmaster! A kind man of sobriety, decency and perfect conduct[326] who had inspired him to read the classics and develop a wide wonder of the world (in quiet times they talked much about virtue and free will and William Paley's blind watchmaker)[327] but when burning timbers trapped his legs he had pushed him away. He was swept up in the panic to get on deck but once there everyone sensed the powder room might burn and explode. Boats were chaotically lowered and all rank and privilege was soon lost. A great wailing of despair arose as men caught fire, and he gagged on the smell of charred flesh. Masts fell and one boy looked up sadly at him as he became trapped. Hopeless. The guns, all loaded with powder, began to fire of their own accord. He made a prayer for salvation just before a jolt threw him onto a burning pile of debris. Shock and pain made him rear up like a guy on fire and he only just managed to find the side of the ship. It had required a supreme effort to jump into the sea and the slap of frigid water almost killed him. An immense explosion was followed by a concussion that hit him like a punch. The thud of wood hitting water above made him realise he was drowning. Hands grabbed his shoulders and brought him back to blessed air where a dazzling scene of deep orange and yellow flames covered everything. Dragged on to the one remaining boat, tears were shed at the awful sight of the ship falling stern first into the depths.

---

326 These words mirror those found in Duncan, 1799, 34.
327 A teleological argument about God's design.

Chapter 6

Arose from out the Azure Main

'Your accent: are you originally from Yorkshire?'

'North Riding.'

'You're not an American then.'

'I am. I married a Yankee girl.'

'Where away?'

'Boston.'

'When?'

'After the last war.'

'How so?'

'I took ship from Plymouth. Weren't no work, see.'

'Likely story. Besides, once a subject always a subject.'[328]

Standing on the deck of HMS *Poictiers*[329] the Yorkshireman, with his big red nose (what the surgeon had told him was *acne rosacea*), balding pate, mutton chops and tobacco-stained teeth, was still in shock. A bluff British lieutenant conducted the interrogation. He thought that despite his rank that man might have served before the mast. A clerk and a boatswain's mate, with cane in hand, stood close by. Beyond them a group of captured Americans stood forlorn, and their ship, the *Wasp*,[330] beaten and sullen.

'I wager there's an R against your name somewhere.'[331]

'No, sir.'

'Ever served on one of His Majesty's warships? Answer true, now.'

'Aye, the *Royal George* that sank off Spithead. I went down with her.'

Rattan hit his shoulders with such force he had to hunch over and let out a grunt.

'Will you fight for King George? No? Then you're made prisoner. Noted this day, 18 October 1812. Next.'

---

328 Taken from Roosevelt, 1882, 2.

329 A 74.

330 The USS *Wasp*, of sixteen 32-pounders and two 12-pounders.

331 Sign for having 'run', or deserted.

As he was taken aside, to stand amongst other captured hands, the prisoner had time to consider how victory had quickly turned to defeat. They were five days out of Delaware, had already lost two men and the jib-boom in a storm, when they spied a small convoy in company of a 16-gun brig called the *Frolic*. It was obvious she was hanging back to allow a convoy to escape. As soon as was wise his captain[332] decided to attack despite heavy seas. They took down their top-gallant yards, close reefed the top-sails and manned the guns.[333] He cheered when Lieutenant Claxton, who was sick, managed to make his way on deck.[334] He had hoped that, unlike what the *Constitution* had done to the *Guerrière*,[335] the enemy would be able to be taken a prize.

At first the *Frolic* had flown Spanish colours[336] while they had shown their own true flag, but as the *Wasp* approached, the enemy brig had hauled up the British ensign and opened fire with guns and muskets. They had returned fire and approached the brig's starboard side. So near did they come to her that his rammer touched the enemy's side when loading his gun, all the while seas pouring in through the gun port. Before long he heard tell how their top-mast and main-topsail yard had fallen across the larboard fore and fore topsail braces,[337] and a few minutes later there was damage to their mizzen topgallant mast. As he struggled with his gun, and the incoming water, someone had shouted that the British were firing high.

They still managed to move ahead and rake the *Frolic* before taking up a position on the British ship's larboard bow. All of their own braces had been shot away so that in such high seas they had worried they might lose every mast. The captain therefore decided to board the enemy lest they lose the prize. So he left his gun to join the boarding party.

By the time he was ready, with cutlass and bludgeon in hand, the two vessels had become entwined. He balked when the *Frolic*'s jib shot overhead, enmeshed in the rigging, with its shadow moving wildly on the deck as they rocked. But it had offered another opportunity to rake them. One American seaman, far too eager, had jumped onto the *Frolic*'s bowsprit[338] despite the captain shouting for him to come back. When Lieutenant Biddle

---

332 Jacob Jones.

333 Palmer, 1814, 22.

334 Lossing, 1869, 450.

335 The USS *Constitution* engaged HMS *Guerrière* 19 August 1812 and damaged her so much she had to be set on fire and blown up.

336 James, 1817, xxii.

337 Palmer, *ibid*, 22.

338 Jack Lang, who had once been pressed to a British warship.

tried to jump over, the boarding party followed. He himself had passed the lieutenant, tied up in loose rigging, to arrive on the enemy fo'c'sle where he was instantly taken aback. It was a charnel house. British seamen lay dead everywhere, their life-blood swilling copiously around their bodies with only three officers alive beside the wheel. They readily surrendered. While he helped secure the ship and hove her off the *Wasp* the British colours were struck by one of their own.

As he stood staring at all the gore, bits of bone and wood strewn along the deck, the surgeon had come across and disappeared below. There were few survivors. As the brig rolled on the heavy seas her two masts groaned and suddenly fell by the board. Rigging, braces and stays went with them. The *Frolic* was a wreck.

They ascertained that the *Wasp* had lost five men dead and five wounded. He himself had a few cuts and bruises to tell a tale but otherwise he was hale and hearty. Ordered to man the *Frolic*, under command of Lieutenant Biddle, he heard they were to make for Charleston. But by then everyone was aware of a large sail hull down on the horizon; a sail suspicious enough for the *Wasp* to investigate. While he cleared away he could see his old ship ready herself for a second action. What a terrible shambles she had looked.

The *Poictiers* soon flew by, fired a shot over their bow, and proceeded to attack the vulnerable *Wasp*. It reminded him of a similar British 74 he had deserted. The *Frolic* was incapable of making sail so he stood amidst the ruined bitts wide-eyed – there was nothing anyone could do. The *Wasp* was boarded, taken and her colours lowered. It did not take long for boats to bring over a raucous band of British tars to deal with her crew. They offered no resistance, were rounded up and taken onboard the *Poictiers*. Everyone knew it might be a long captivity.

As his old ship-mates were interrogated, and his officers entertained, a fellow American whispered in his ear: 'We'll be for Bermuda, no doubt.' 'Aye,' he replied, 'or a British jail.' They both gulped at that thought.

The USS *Wasp* (18) was taken into the British service, renamed HMS *Loup Cervier* and later HMS *Peacock*. Despite that, 'The victory of the *Wasp* over the *Frolic* – the result of the first combat between the vessels of the two nations of a force nearly equal – occasioned much exaltation in the United States.'[339] There circulated a ditty that ended with the refrain, 'And he writhed and he groaned as if torn with the colic; And long shall John Bull

---

339 Lossing, *ibid.*

rue the terrible day, He met the American *Wasp* on a *Frolic*.'[340] On arrival at Bermuda the prisoners were exchanged and Captain Jones and Lieutenant Biddle were both lauded upon their return home.

Seven days after the action between the *Wasp*, *Frolic* and *Poictiers*, the *United States* (32) fought the *Macedonian* (38), and whereas the British ship was considered to be an excellent sailer, 'every shot told with deadly and destructive effect upon [her]... and even yet, with nearly a hundred shots in her hull, her lower guns under water, in a tempestuous sea, and a third of her crew either killed or wounded, Captain Carden fought his ship... boarding was rendered impossible.'[341] She was forced to strike her colours and suffered 36 dead and 68 wounded; the *United States* suffered 5 killed and 7 wounded.[342]

The *Constitution* (32) met the *Java* (38) off the Brazils on 28 December 1812. After the private signal was not answered the American ship closed, thereby separating the British ship from another strange sail, and both warships offered broadsides and played cat and mouse to try to rake the other. The American ship had her wheel shot away[343] and the British warship lost her bowsprit, jib-boom, foremast, main-topmast, gaff, spanker-boom and eventually her main mast. In two hours the *Java* was a wreck. They were far from America so after the *Java*'s crew had been taken prisoner the wreck was burned. Those taken hostage were landed and parolled. They comprised the usual assortment of naval officers, Royal Marines, warrant officers and seamen, officers of the land service and eight civilian passengers. The US Navy had seriously embarrassed the Royal Navy.

At this time many foreign servicemen were incarcerated in British prisons. Mostly French and Spanish, they were joined, from 1812 onwards, by Americans. The War of 1812 lasted until 18 February 1815 and was the result of long-term grievances held by the USA during a period of peace with Britain that many considered a mere truce. In British circles there had lingered a 'spirit of unextinguished animosity towards the United States'.[344] After 1793 the Navy blockaded France, Holland, Spain and parts of Italy to the detriment of American commerce. British warships apprehended and forcibly searched foreign bottoms. George Canning spoke to Parliament on 18 February 1813 stating that, for him, the British 'are by ancient and

340 *Harper's New Monthly Magazine*, 1862, 170.
341 Roger, 1856, 193.
342 Clark, 1813, 157/158.
343 *Ibid*, 163.
344 Armstrong, 1836, 9.

unquestioned usage, and by the law of nations, as they are now understood, in the possession of the right of search.'[345]

It was not only search that had caused dismay. American seamen had been 'forcibly seized, dragged on board [British] ships of war and made to fight her battles'[346] The French did the same: James Emott delivered a speech to the House of Representatives on 12 January 1813 in which he said, 'we have the names of upwards of twenty American citizens, taken out of American vessels, on the high seas, by French privateers... ; and that Henry Doughty, an American, was impressed at sea, from the American brig Elsa, by the French frigates Lapancey and Thetis. I could instance other cases, but these are sufficient to show, that neither the claim nor the exercise of it is peculiar to the British.'[347] But the numbers taken by British naval ships were greater. Diplomatic forbearance had been pursued by the USA until she declared war against the Britain on 18 June 1812.

One issue raised by this conflict was the status of naturalised seamen and soldiers. If a British man or woman had previously renounced their British citizenship in favour of the United States, and were later taken prisoners by the British, what was their status? According to the US government, Britain no longer held any rights or duties over them; that although they had taken up arms against their birth country they should not be considered traitors. *Cobbett's Political Register* of 1813 laid out what was a widespread assertion of some British commentators at this time: that allegiance was 'unalienable',[348] in that 'every man continues, to the day of his death, a subject of the state wherein he was born... that, of course, any act of his, in open hostility, and especially of arms-bearing against his native state, if it be a voluntary act on his part, is an act coming under the description of *treason.*' The article argued how this was not the case with the War of 1812, for to be considered naturalised a person had to have lived five years or more within the USA, or be married to an American, and he or she would not have moved abroad during peace knowing there would later be a war against the British. They risked a long sea journey and an uncertain period of settlement to make a better life for themselves. The article also stressed how Americans should not be treated in the same way as armed French

---

345 *The Parliamentary Debates Vol XXIV*, 1813, 637.
346 Armstrong, *ibid*, 12.
347 Emott, 1813, 25. There was a French brig called *La Pensée*.
348 *Cobbett's Political Register*, 1813,163. He writes against an article that appeared in *The Courier*.

émigrés; that the British army and navy were themselves comprised of foreigners, most of whom had not been naturalised.

But the threat remained that an American taken prisoner could feasibly be accused of treason, or misprision of treason, and under British law punishment was gruesome. For treason the guilty could be 'hanged for some time, cut down before they are dead, having their bowels ripped out while they are yet alive, then having their heads chopped off, and their bodies cut each into four quarters, to be placed at the disposal of the King.'[349] For misprision of treason, where someone conceals a traitor, punishment was 'forfeiture of goods and chattels and imprisonment for the life of the party.'[350]

On arrival in Britain (at Portsmouth, Chatham or Plymouth) a prisoner became the concern of the naval Transport Office and his status and citizenship recorded in minute detail. If he arrived at Plymouth as a commissioned officer he received parole and was marched inland to reside at Ashburton. Once there he received a small allowance, was allowed to walk a small distance from the town each day, but was expected to return and remain indoors at night.[351] If a non-commissioned officer, seaman, marine or soldier was taken at sea and arrived in Plymouth he was incarcerated in one of two hulks that lay in the Hamoaze – the *Hector* and *Brave* that 'lie about two miles from Plymouth, well moored by chain moorings' – or in Mill Prison. He received a 'coarse and worthless hammock, with a thin coarse bed-sack, with at most not more than three or four pounds of flops or chopped rags, one thin coarse and sleazy blanket'.

An account by Charles Andrews, taken prisoner in the War of 1812, stated how prisoners were not allowed to remain idle. Roused each morning by the invalided guard if they were kept on a hulk they had to heave their hammocks up to the weather deck and receive daily tasks to clean or store the hulk. For food they received some bread, 'half a pound of beef, including the bone, one-third of an ounce of salt, and the same quantity of barley, with one or two turnips per man.' Two days a week this was substituted by salt fish, bread and potatoes. No alcohol or candles were ever allowed, no unauthorised boat could approach a hulk, and no unauthorised person enter a prison. Their letters were restricted.

---

349 *Ibid,* 165. An old law on the books, seldom used but always possible. In the Treason Act of 1814 [54 Geo. III c. 146] the form of death was altered to hanging then posthumous quartering. Beheading for treason remained on the books until 1973.

350 *Cobbett's Complete Collection of State Trials*, 1819, 435.

351 Andrews, 1852, 6. Further quotes from the same source.

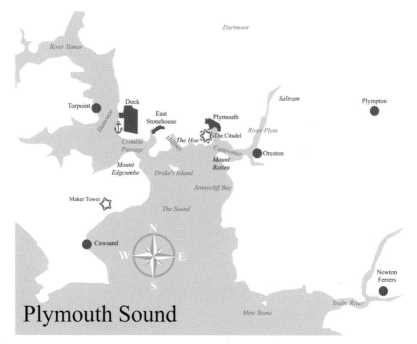

Plymouth Sound

Commonly referred to as 'Plymouth', this West Country town comprised three separate conurbations: Plymouth, East Stonehouse and Dock... the 'Second Port of the Kingdom'. Settled on land between the rivers Tamar and Plym whose waters met to create Plymouth Sound, a large body of water that allowed entrance and exit to the sea. Outside this sound lay the chops of the Channel and France just beyond. (Map by the author)

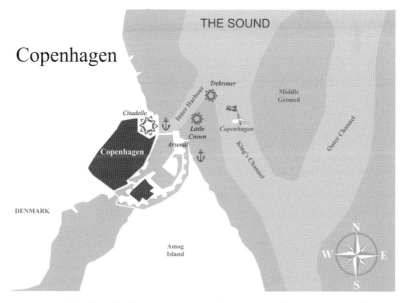

Discussions with the ship's master centred on possible directions they might approach Copenhagen. Copenhagen was Denmark's main naval arsenal, with fearsome batteries. It proved to be a difficult approach. (Map by the author)

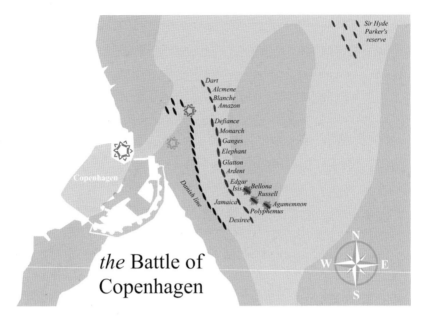

the Battle of Copenhagen

The Edgar eventually anchored by the stern opposite that fifth enemy hulk. Like all others of the British division her prow faced north, while the Danes' prows faced south. Sir Hyde Parker's reserve waited and could merely observe. (Map by the author)

The Baltic

The entrance by the British fleet into the Baltic, then little known to most of her officers and masters, added to the renown of Nelson. The sound that fronted Copenhagen was the first, and major, obstacle the Royal Navy had to confront in this theatre. (Map by the author)

The English Channel

Flat-boats from the previous conflict resided along the enemy channel coast and France had strengthened her shore defences. The threat to England was real, and people lived in fear of an invasion. (Map by the author)

You know, where they float masts to keep 'em from cracking? Masts were vital for ships of the era, and their supply from source to completion was of national importance. (title: "Working on a Mast 1803," by archivist, Adobe Stock)

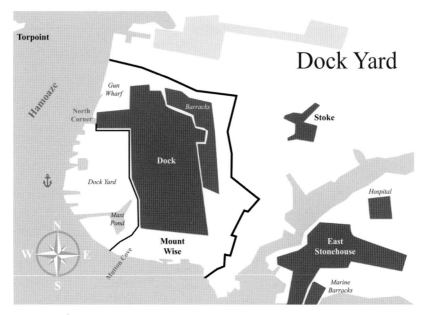

At Dock the Royal Navy maintained a large and vibrant shipyard. Royal Navy ships and vessels could lay in comfort in the wide basin known as the Hamoaze which fronts the naval yard. In the age of sail it was oftentimes difficult to depart into the sound. (Map by the author)

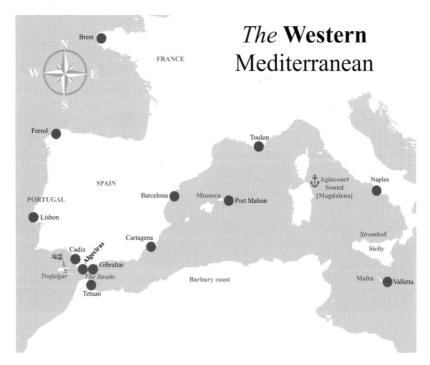

But war came nonetheless and Nelson boarded the Victory at Portsmouth, on 18 May 1803, to sail to the Mediterranean. He was well used to its waters and once again would chase a French fleet. (Map by the author)

Eager British ships made sail for their foe, To halt their designs and bring them woe, French and Spanish hopes halted and checked, Their ships captured, burnt, or made pitiful wrecks. One of many line of battleships, the *Victory* became the most famous Royal Navy ship thanks to the Battle of Trafalgar. (title: "Sailing Ships - Victory," by archivist, Adobe Stock)

Nelson appeared on deck 'dressed as usual in his admiral's frock-coat, bearing on his left breast four stars of different orders, which he always wore with his common apparel.' A sometimes difficult and vainglorious man, Nelson inspired admiration in those men [and possibly women] who served with him. His loss was keenly felt. (title: "Lord Nelson" by Tony Baggett, Adobe Stock)

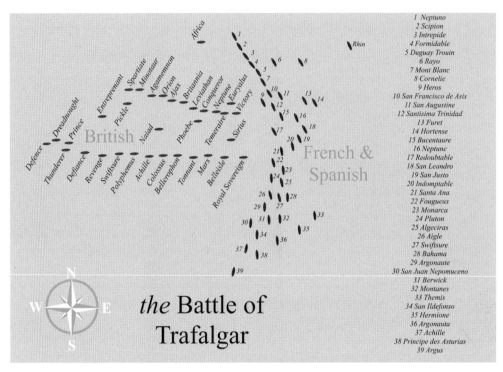

Two days later, seven leagues off Cape Trafalgar, the British closed in two columns in very light winds against the enemy that had formed up in an irregular line, convex as a crescent to leeward. The battle that followed was seen as a key moment in British and world history. (Map by the author)

Vice Admiral Collingwood, in command of the lee column upon the Royal Sovereign, wrote in his dispatch of 22 October that 'in leading down to their centre, I had both their van and rear abaft the beam.' At the Battle of Trafalgar Collingwood's and Nelson's columns broke the enemy line in two separate places. (title: "An engraved illustration image of the Battle of Trafalgar 1805, from a vintage Victorian book dated 1884 that is no longer in copyright" by Tony Baggett, Adobe Stock)

Nelson, who refused to hide his 'insignia,' was an open and visible target to 'musketeers in the tops of the enemy's ships'. Trafalgar was both a national triumph and tragedy. (title: "Admiral Nelson's Death at Trafalgar Battle - 1805," by Erica Guilane-Nachez, Adobe Stock)

A musket ball hit him in the left breast and he died after two hours. Nelson's death inspired much print, countless illustrations and many poems. (title: "An engraved illustration image of the death of Admiral Lord Horatio Nelson on HMS *Victory*, from a Victorian book dated 1884 that is no longer in copyright," by Tony Baggett, Adobe Stock)

For many people of this era their beliefs and consciences resulted in a disgust of the slave trade. Their Golden Rule was do unto others as you would have others do unto you. William Wilberforce was one of the leading lights to end the slave trade. (title: "William Wilberforce" by Georgios Kollidas, Adobe Stock)

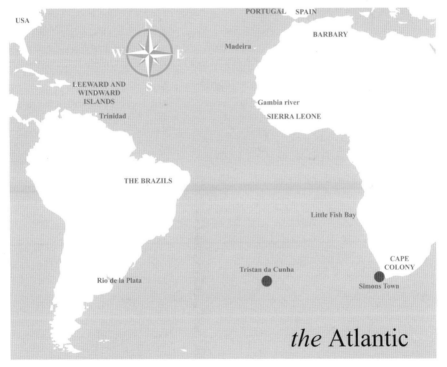

the Atlantic

It was a time when the French were not as diminished as the British public knew or liked to admit so the remit of two warships, Solebay (32) and Derwent (18), was given to patrol the African coast roughly from the river Gambia in the north to Little Fish Bay in the south. Their aim was to restrict the African slave trade. (Map by the author)

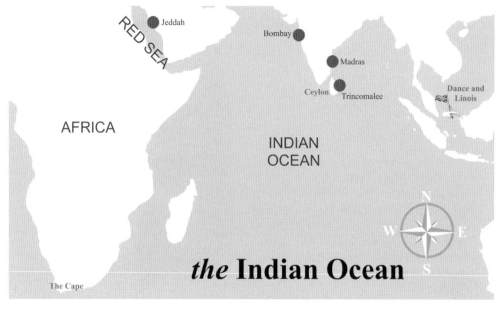

'Admiral Linois, if you recall, was a rum fellow. His ship, the Marengo, had with her an accompaniment of three frigates and a brig and he tried to harry a British merchant fleet.' The war extended far beyond Europe, even to the 'China Sea'. (Map by the author)

He thought to himself, how many wrecks have there been in this war? How many warships and men lost to the sea? With limited charts and the vagaries of the wind, the Royal Navy suffered many wrecks in this war. (title: "Shipwreck - Naufrage - 19th," by Erica Guilane-Nachez, Adobe Stock)

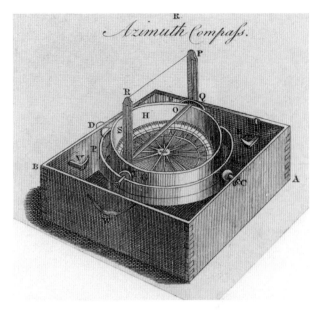

Azimuth Compass.

What kept him active were his thoughts, books and periodicals on hydrographic and nautical themes, old instruments of navigation and an antique globe. Instruments such as the azimuth compass were vital for navigation. (title: "Azimuth Compass. Date: 1797" by archivist, Adobe Stock)

The Penguin *was fine enough, less than two years old, but seventeen of her crew were boys, many of the older men had been previously discharged and most of the younger lot pressed into service.* In an ideal world most of the junior hands were youths, or young men, best able to adapt to the rigours of the sea. (title: "Heaving the Lead. Date: 18th century" by archivist, Adobe Stock)

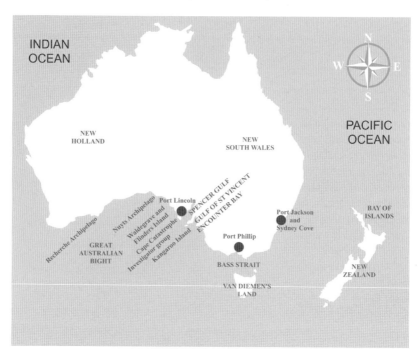

HMS *Investigator was active from 1801 to 1803 (until considered unseaworthy and paid off at Plymouth in 1806). In her brief time she surveyed the southern coast of Australia.* New South Wales then extended all the way from Bass Strait to Torres Strait in the far north. (Map by the author)

The speaker told them, our Master Attendant believes thirty-six ships of the line would be so protected, a great gain to England! They would be so much closer to the enemy at Brest and we would no longer have to convey stores overland to Torbay, for as you all know the fleet often has to shy away from the dangers of the Sound to anchor over there. Until the breakwater was completed Torbay was the better option for a naval fleet to ride at anchor. (title: "Fleet at Torbay. Date: 1805" by archivist, Adobe Stock)

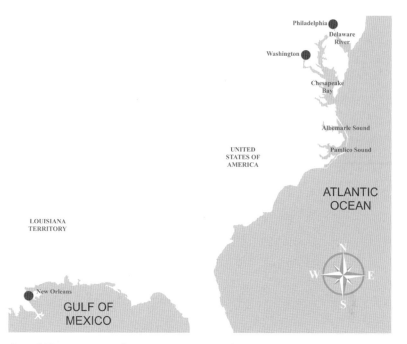

The Royal Navy continued to put pressure on the United States through blockade. The British patrolled a large area, from Long Island Sound in the north to Pamlico Sound in the south. (Map by the author)

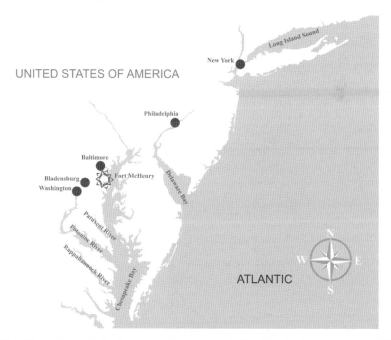

In 1814 Vice Admiral Cochrane took over both the North American and West Indies station and brought together a squadron based on Bermuda and Halifax. They penetrated the Chesapeake and landed troops to burn Washington. The White House was also torched. (Map by the author)

In 1802 the Charlotte Dundas demonstrated the practical use of a steam-vessel. The use of such vessels accelerated as the war came to an end, namely for commercial use. Eventually, the Royal Navy introduced some to her own fleets. (title: "Charlotte Dundas. Date 1802" from archivist, Adobe Stock)

The widow and her daughter were part of a sheltered human archipelago set amidst a wide and destitute country. War made many widows, and for women the wait and uncertainty was difficult. Especially for those of low income. (title: "Costume - G R Ward circa 1815. Date: circa 1815" by archivist, Adobe Stock)

One key aspect of the means by which fleets conducted themselves in battle was the use of signals. A range of flags in combination with pennants, jacks and guns allowed commanders to order quite detailed commands by day. One of the most recognisable flags to civilians would have been the white ensign. (title: "White Ensign," by andyh12, Adobe Stock)

Napoleon claimed that he had boarded the Bellerophon (74) a free man and not a prisoner. He thought himself 'the guest of England'. His first step on the deck of a British ship was the signal that the long naval war was over. (title: "Napoleon Exiled -begining19th century" by Erica Guilane-Nachez, Adobe Stock)

Napoleon stood high above them on the deck of the 74, his stature small and squat, and he was definitely on show. The crowd gave him the same respect they would an exhibit in a ceremonial levee. It was a memorable scene at the end of a very long war. (title: "Napoleon in Plymouth Sound" by Jules Giradet, oil on canvas © The Box [Plymouth Museums Galleries Archives])

The Bellerophon was made a prison hulk in 1819 off Sheerness. Many old and famous ships ended their life as a prison hulk. (title: "Prison ships (hulks), Britain (from Das Heller- Magazin, May 10, 1834" by Juulijs, Adobe Stock)

At certain times prisoners of war were exchanged. For example, on 13 September 1798 Rupert George, John Marsh, Ambrose Serle and John Schank of the Transport Office signed a document pertaining to a 'Cartel for the Exchange of Prisoners of War between Great Britain and France'.[352] France was first to send over, via a cartel vessel, 'a number of British prisoners, with the proportion of five officers to one hundred men'.[353] The British would do the same, and both belligerents repeat the process until either party decided to stop. Men incapable of service, and boys under the age of 10, were exchanged but not counted in exchange totals: 'Surgeons, surgeons' mates, pursers (or *aides-commissaires*), pursers' stewards (or *commis aux vivres*), secretaries, chaplains, and schoolmasters... and also passengers not of the sea or land service, but shall be immediately set at liberty, to return to their respective countries.'[354] Released prisoners were expected to be on parole. A table of equivalent ranks of officers was given. During the exchange an agreed amount of bread, beef and beer was to be provided per prisoner.

A common complaint made by prisoners was that they were not permitted to manufacture what might have made them money to better themselves and their diet. Andrews thought it a ploy to make fellow compatriots seek employment with the Royal Navy. But prisoners made small items like spoons and punch ladles. In a number of publications of 1824 and 1825 a widely circulated article considered the nature of Frenchmen and concluded that they could 'accommodate themselves more readily to circumstances',[355] that when cast upon a 'desolate island' they would take a cocoa nut and carve upon it an image of Bonaparte or make 'clay models of everything upon the island'. He stated, 'I have known a French prisoner spend every leisure hour, for many years, in manufacturing a line-of-battle ship, out of the little splinters of bone which he found in the soup... . That a French prisoner of war, a good seaman, (for a Frenchman,) should employ himself, year after year, in miniature ship-building; substituting beef bone for oak timber, and converting what other men would hardly have had the patience or the power to make a tooth-pick of, into accurate and beautiful machinery.'

Mill Prison, named after windmills that had once stood on the site, sat on the west end of the Hoe towards Plymouth Marsh and overlooked Mill

---

352 *A Collection of State Papers relative to the War against France,* 1799, 338 to 340.
353 *Ibid,* 338.
354 *Ibid,* 339.
355 *The Atheneum,* 1825, 141. Following quotes of Frenchmen and their 'arts' from this source.

Bay. Built in the time of Queen Anne it had a large open space enclosed by a high wall and three buildings, one being a cook-room. One building was 'one hundred feet long and twenty wide, situated at the north end of the yard... two stories high, built of stone, and without windows on the north front... the commissary's office... stood at the west, having no windows in the east end.'[356] On 9 August 1760 some 150 French prisoners escaped the place after undermining a wall;[357] most were later apprehended but sixteen disappeared.

Andrew Sherburne wrote an informative memoir of his capture, transfer and time spent in this prison during the 1780s. Although extraordinary, and not fully indicative of other prisoners' experiences then and in the War of 1812, his time in England was. When aged 16 he was captured and taken to Placentia, Newfoundland, where he was eventually placed onboard the *Duchess of Cumberland* (16), being told he was for St John's, the capital of the province, for a prison ship and possible exchange. At sea the weather turned foul, her officers ignored a local fisherman's advice and soon ran aground on the eastern side of Cape St Mary's. Sherburne survived the wreck on a rugged, 'iron-bound' shore. With other survivors he walked nine days to find a small port, where he received some food and drink, before continuing on to Placentia. There he recovered over four weeks.

Sherburne said that men like himself feared impressment 'as a flock of sheep... dread the appearance of a wolf'[358] and when the *Fairy* (16) came in he was sent onboard despite complaining he was a prisoner of war and would not serve against his country. He hid in the ship's cable tier but was soon roused out to do duty by the boatswain's rattan cane (he was befriended by the carpenter and given light duties). When the ship reached St John's it was found the cartel had already sailed.

He arrived in Plymouth in November 1781. He was shocked to find a lot of women allowed onboard, for 'it was not common for the men to be allowed to go on shore, to stay overnight',[359] and he spent several weeks in the sound. He was not sent ashore for his status was deemed to be that of a British sailor. When a new captain took command he had an audience with him and stated openly he was an American prisoner and wished to go to prison. So, accompanied by a midshipman and marines with fixed bayonets, he was taken by boat to the Hamoaze and placed on the guard-ship

---

356 McClintock, 1881, 266.
357 *The British Chronologist*, 1775, 329.
358 Sherburne, 1831, 70.
359 Sherburne, *ibid,* 74. Further quotes regarding his story from the same source.

Dunkirk (74). He considered this ship a 'floating hell' where drinking and debauchery were rife and everything bar his clothes were stolen. He did meet an old colleague, William Lamb, who had been pressed, had deserted and been pressed again; the second time he used a false name because if found out he would hang 'at the yard arm'.

Over successive days other American prisoners arrived on board, together with those pressed by several independent gangs quartered on the ship. Many pressed men arrived 'shockingly bruised and mangled'. After a while Sherburne feared an administrative error had him slated for another warship so he made three complaints until sent ashore with twelve prisoners to face a court of Admiralty. Americans sometimes had to argue they were not British subjects, but he appears not to have been asked, and was committed to Old Mill Prison for 'rebellion, piracy, and high treason on his Britannic Majesty's high seas'. It was then January, no doubt cold, and Sherburne had few clothes to keep warm. After a march of a mile to the prison he entered a yard near the cookhouse, found a sentinel on continual guard with 'old Aunt Anna', a sutler, before going through a guarded inner gate to the prison proper. Inside he found numerous fellow Americans.

Years later, in 1799, George Lipscomb made a tour of the West Country and visited the prison. On one hand he observed that 'notwithstanding the accounts propagated to the contrary, we were happy to find them [the prisoners] in possession of many comforts as well as every necessary,' but on the other hand, 'We were informed that a fever had lately made great ravages of the prison… when we walked round the south west wall… the stench of the sewers was intolerable.'[360] Lipscomb hoped that authorities would take heed of that.

The effect of imprisonment on the minds of foreign soldiers and sailors can only be imagined. Violence must have been commonplace. On 1 August 1807 a Spaniard stabbed to death a man blocking his entrance to the cook-room at Mill Prison; he was hanged for 'wilful murder'.[361] A prisoner was said to have died from starvation in the 'hospital… having actually gambled away eight days' provisions. So inveterate is the itch of the prisoners for gambling, that they make billiard tables on the earth.'[362] The *Annual Register* for 1801 stated that their agent, Mr Claverton, had taken away their gaming tables.[363]

---

360 *The Monthly Review*, 1801, 154.
361 Urban, 1807, 879.
362 Buck, 1805, 108.
363 *The Annual Register*, 1801, 31.

As reported by the admiralty to Parliament on 1 February 1815, '2,548 impressed American seamen, who refused to serve against their country, were imprisoned in 1812... 3,300 men claiming to be American subjects were serving in the British navy in January, 1811.'[364] Andrews thought 700 Americans were incarcerated in Plymouth by April 1813 and believed that authorities, fearful of a mass escape, landed prisoners held onboard the *Hector* hulk to march them seventeen miles inland to Dartmoor prison. With so many men confined in dirty conditions disease was all too common. An outbreak of measles occurred at Mill Prison between 14 May and 18 June 1812 amongst French prisoners. A Dr Lockyer of Plymouth[365] reported his use of 'cold affusion' at the prison hospital and a similar remedy for a bout of 148 cases of measles at Dartmoor prison. Charles Andrews named 190 Americans who died in that prison between April 1813 and February 1815, from Henry Alligo of New York to Sola of Massachusetts and William Young of North Carolina.

As to the conduct of the War of 1812 the United States Navy gained notable victories at sea and appeared to have reached a high pinnacle. The British admiralty failed at first to send more powerful ships to the North America station. Instead it was assumed that British spirit and dash would be enough to restore prestige. They 'continued to send slow-sailing brigs and ill-armed sloops of war, for the protection of large fleets of merchantmen, with valuable cargoes, while the frigates of the enemy... were faster than British seventy-fours, and were equal to British ships... in armament.'[366] British warships were soon barred from engaging heavier American frigates, that had 'scantling and armament corresponding to their own seventy-fours',[367] if ever found alone.

People began to ask difficult questions. Canning said that the USA desired an end to paper blockades, those 'blockades' only in name and not backed up with ships. He believed America 'had an itch for war with this country, and they were determined to have it,'[368] despite having only '1,000 soldiers, four or five frigates... to guard an extent of coast of 1,500 miles, and a revenue of only two millions and a half dollars, I think, or thereabouts... . Could a nation so circumstanced venture upon a war with the mighty empire of Great Britain, with the most distant prospect

---

364 Footnote in Roosevelt, 1882, 42.
365 *The Edinburgh Medical and Surgical Journal*, 1813, 407.
366 Roger, *ibid*, 195.
367 Auchinleck, 1855, 65. Scantling refers to the strength of a section of a ship.
368 *The Parliamentary Debates Vol XXIV*, 1813, 637.

of success?' Unluckily it did. 'The unwelcome truth cannot be concealed. Two out of these four or five frigates have captured two frigates from the British navy… . It is no answer to say, that our navy is immense, but that it is proportionally extended on the different stations. I complain not of the naval department, but of the policy which controuled its operations… I do not attribute the slightest blame to our gallant sailors; they always do their duty… *It cannot be too deeply felt that the sacred spell of the invincibility of the British navy was broken by those unfortunate captures.*'[369] He added that he hoped the war would not end before the Royal Navy had regained 'the character of our naval superiority'.[370]

Many people who heard, or later read, Canning's speech would have agreed with him along the lines of *what was the point of a naval superpower if it could not impose its will? What did it mean to be the senior service, in command of vast expenditure, if such a colossal fleet was not enough to beat a small navy?*

The American navy comprised frigates built out of their Naval Act of 1794. Ostensibly to protect their sea trade from Barbary pirates there was ordered a permanent establishment of 'Four ships of forty-four guns each, and two of thirty-six'.[371] Later, a further six 74s were ordered but never built. When launched the two 44s were larger than any British frigate. As William James pointed out they were large enough that in heavy weather, when a double-deck warship had to close her lower ports because of the waves, they could compete on almost equal terms.

The construction of the American warships proved insightful. Anything new was adopted by their shipwrights, despite the costs, and 'There were no contractors, to make a hard bargain pay, by deteriorating the quality of the job… not a plank was shifted, nor a long-bolt driven, without the scrutinizing eye of one of the captains or commodores.'[372] The ships were commanded by the same men who oversaw their construction and it was very much in their interests to attain the best possible build. The timber used had been noted in the first ever *Naval Chronicle* in 1799, a popular read for all British naval officers, when it reported how an American committee resolved to 'secure a sufficient quantity of timber, and to have it in readiness for building ships of war. To effect this… it would be necessary to purchase a forest of live oak and red cedar. And having good timber secured, no nation on earth could

---

369 *Ibid*, 643. Author's italics.
370 *Ibid*.
371 Kimball, 1835, 9.
372 James, *ibid*, 3.

build better ships than the United States.'[373] Southern live oak was almost imperishable and extremely tough so that when these frigates, what William James called 'line-of-battleships in disguise', eventually faced British warships, their design, construction, armament and strength shocked Royal Navy officers. It also unsettled many British civilians.

In June 1812 a disgruntled out of work labourer from Newton Ferrers, oftentimes involved in the smuggling trade, offered his labour for a new national enterprise. He walked to Plymouth to join a large crowd that gathered to hear about John Rennie and the proposed Plymouth breakwater. They were told how ships currently could not anchor in the Sound, but if protection was made it would render the place more favourable than Torbay or Falmouth.[374] He knew enough of the sea to recognise that a proper shelter in the sound would allow a ship to sail out with an easterly wind better than any other western port; that it would allow many ships to anchor in the sound ready for an enemy incursion.

The crowd was told how surveys had been conducted since 1806 to the point that a mile-long breakwater with east and west passages was to be built. The speaker told them, *our Master Attendant believes thirty-six ships of the line would be so protected, a great gain to England! They would be so much closer to the enemy at Brest and we would no longer have to convey stores overland to Torbay, for as you all know the fleet often has to shy away from the dangers of the Sound to anchor over there.* Someone dared ask how much it would cost. £1,500,000 was the reply. Everyone present was staggered at the sum and he personally doubted such a monstrous thing could ever be constructed in the middle of the sea. But what if the enemy should descend, and if authorities were dumb enough to pay him then so be it.

Therefore on 12 August 1812 he took to a boat with a handful of men and sailed out to the Shovel and Carlos Rocks to deposit the first stone. It was a beautiful day and a whole procession of boats, full of worthies and bedecked with flags and the Royal Standard,[375] went with them. He was told that Lord Keith, naval captains, captains of marines and black coated civilians were all in attendance, but he recognised none of them nor did he care to. He detested *those riotous and roguish knaves.* When the rock was released it made an immense splash, a noticeable wave and disappeared into the deep. There was a great cheer and guns were fired. He grimaced throughout.

---

373 *Naval Chronicle*, 1799, 331.
374 *Cobbett's Parliamentary Debates Vol XXI*, 1812, 1311.
375 Granville, 1825, 24.

At first he was mostly at work in Oreston, in the Cattewater, to build a quay wall there and a crane to load stone and rubble onto boats, as well as cut the ground for rails that would bring limestone rocks from the quarries. The rocks were to be one-and-a-half to two tons each. He returned to the breakwater on 20 March 1813 after rubble had been 'brought to within 5 feet of low water of spring tides.'[376] Boats laden with rubble sailed out to dump their loads at directed spots and within ten days it had begun to show above the water. By August 1813 it had risen enough that, for the first time, workers could land on it.

The labourer was impressed with the width of the breakwater, some seventy yards, that in his head he had not been able to imagine. There already formed a slope from the surface of the sea to the top of the wall. However, the works at Oreston were an awful place for the faint of heart. He knew of one man whose hand was crushed beyond recognition by a rock that slipped in transit, and a drunkard was cut in two when a taut rope snapped.

By early autumn 1813 he was working the breakwater full time, arriving in the morning and departing before dusk apart from times of high tide and storms. By then cut stone was being delivered for the top of the wall. They were also to be used to build a lighthouse. Together with simple rubble they arrived by specially designed boats that sailed up to a buoy, turned stern on, opened two rear ports and delivered the rocks from within. Each delivery required around an hour to complete, dependent on the state of the sea.

He was a man of pure muscle with a wide barrel chest, and stood extremely tall with a face like an enraged cherub. He received the name 'Zoilus';[377] his daily complaints about work, multitudes of pox-ridden sailors and their bawdy-house liaisons, the cost of necessities, worries about the war and the number of prisoners exhausted everyone. Years of rough alcohol and fear of capture had taken a toll and his account was long overdue.

One cold and miserable day, he landed with an itinerant worker from Taunton who seemed confused as to why the breakwater was being built. Zoilus told him how, in 1797, there had been a calamity so bad it had been written about in the papers. The sea rose amid a storm and floated off '40 to 50 vessels... lying aground, moored head and stern... and the reflux of the sea carried near twenty fishing smacks, sloops, and barges, with a great number of boats, upwards of a mile, into the Sound, at the rate of ten or twelve knots; soon after which another bore came on and

---

376 *The Mechanics' Magazine*, 1848, 423.
377 A fierce critic.

brought several of them back into the Pool, others into Catwater, and some were drifted near the rocks below the citadel.'[378] The traveller from Taunton was shocked, being unused to the sea, and looked with suspicion upon the waves that lapped the seaward side of the breakwater. Zoilus explained how one sloop had been dragged under the toll bridge at Stonehouse. *Her main-mast and bowsprit were carried clean away, which I saw with my own eyes. See then what we're about? This here wall will stop that.*

One day, when they loitered beside a crane on the breakwater, he told the labourer from Taunton how he had helped build Dartmoor prison. *A dreary place best forgotten.* The 'grand Prison of War'[379] and newly built town[380] *named in honour of the Prince of Wales*, sat amongst bogs and hills *but I much prefer the sea.*

With the breakwater there was much to find impressive. *The foreman, he thinks he knows much but he don't realise how much rubble we need to make this here wall. But I do. Want to know? More than three million tons. Enough to build a tower to the moon!*[381] Foreign prisoners and the war were perennial topics of conversation. *And I heard tell how some Yankee prisoners in Dartmoor made banknotes that allowed them to buy their way out. So brazen faced were they, they got clean away to Ireland and now fight against our lice-ridden warships.*[382] *They no doubt plan to attack this business of Rennie's, so mind you don't fall captive. Stick by me and there'll be no irons for you.*

Zoilus sometimes went to Dock to help load up necessaries and return to the breakwater with the boat (for the foreman wanted to get rid of him as much as possible). Once, in December 1813, he awaited the arrival of the boat at the landing steps of the dockyard. The persistent rain made the white marble flagstones shimmer.[383] On a false pretext, he managed to sneak away for a drink or three at a local tavern. It was only the difficult journey back that sobered him up, otherwise he would have hit the foreman on his return. Instead he was merely irritable and peevish and no one noticed. He mumbled so that all could hear: 'The Yankees have showed us a thing

378 Urban, 1797, 705.

379 *The Annual Register*, 1806, 140.

380 Princetown.

381 In total 3,620,444 tons of rubble was used with 2,512,696 cubic feet of masonry. It was said to have originated as an idea with Earl St Vincent.

382 *Cobbett's Political Register*, 1819, 785.

383 Hoxland, 1796, 17. Dock town was known for her streets paved with marble that shimmered white when it rained.

or two. Lake Erie, what a disgrace. Two ships, two brigs, a schooner and a sloop all lost.[384] What a blow. I bet those bigwigs in the admiralty are worried.'

The worker from Taunton asked him, 'How so?'

'See that warship over there? When was the last time she went into action? I'll wager not since Nelson's time. All the boys on board do nought but make salutes, keep the brightwork clean, and stand around like ornaments.[385] Pitiful. She couldn't beat a well manned ship the Americans have built, not with the soft wood she is made of. Our navy has become old and careless.'

Taunton tried to argue otherwise, but Zoilus felt himself on firm ground. 'Listen good. You've seen all those idle, well-fed, soldiers on the Hoe. Nowadays the army takes all the best men. The navy, what reckons herself senior of old, gets only gallows-men and lowlights. And don't think the Royal Marines have it easy neither. No, it's those battalion-marines who cop all the good men now, so that only young lads become ship marines. I tell you, it's all change, and for the worse. The wooden-wall? Bah!'

Many people argued for change, such as William Cobbett, who in a letter 'on the American War' suggested improvements. He felt the naval profession both honourable and of great importance to Britain, that 'it would require the greatest skill and most undaunted courage on their part to enable them to maintain the dominion of the seas',[386] but nevertheless urged implementation of an improved mode of promotion and distribution of prize money. As for the USA, the war demonstrated she could compete, ship for ship, with the British, and that worried many.

Time moved on and the work persisted so that by 1814 there had been deposited more than 230,000 tons of rubble at the site of the breakwater.[387] Zoilus and Taunton were then part of more than three hundred quarrymen and labourers who worked the project. They reported to their foreman who

---

384 Palmer, 1814, 297: It stated, 'Statement of the Force of the British Squadron. Ship Detroit, 19 guns, one on a pivot, and 2 howitzers; Queen Charlotte, 17... a schooner Lady Prevost, 13... brig Hunter, 10... sloop Little Belt, 3... schr. Chippeway, 1... and 2 swivels - 63 guns.' The force of the US Squadron was 'Brig Lawrence, 20 guns, Niagara, 20... Caledonia, 3... schooner Ariel, 4... Scorpion, 2... Somers, 2... and 2 swivels... sloop Trippe, 1... schooner Tigress, 1... Porcupine, 1... - 54 guns.' The British force was part of the Provincial Marine and not the Royal Navy although they were often manned by naval personnel.

385 A criticism made by James.

386 *The Atheneum*, 1825, 221.

387 Granville, *ibid*, 30.

in turn reported to a superintendent. Ninety seamen worked the boats that ferried them back and forth with masons, blacksmiths, carpenters and other labourers. In the winter their faces were red-raw with the cold, while in the summer red-raw with the sun. They came to appreciate how the breakwater did in fact break the water and provide shelter in its lee. Fishermen gathered there daily before venturing beyond, while their sheer vessel[388] lurked nearby.

On 31 March 1814 both the Emperor of Russia and the Duke of Wellington entered Paris, and by May Bonaparte was on Elba for his first exile. In Plymouth there were church peals, addresses and celebrations, for the war in Europe appeared to have come to an end, though the conflict with America persisted. British troops were transferred from Europe to Canada.

One day in late 1814 Taunton asked Zoilus why he so hated the navy. Zoilus looked up, trawl in hand, and quietly told his story. 'I ran see, off a warship more than fifteen years back. I was a boy amidst a den of disease, drunkenness and death.[389] What vices they all had. There were men onboard with the smell of correction houses about them, and more than a few lunatics. They preyed on the youngsters and in the presence of some I feared for my life. So I jumped. I can swim, see, and the waters at the Nore aren't too bad when the tides are right. I hid, covered in mud, for days. Half-starved but free. I managed to clean up and make my way inland. No one took any notice for I was a lad. Afore I knew it I had found work as a labourer and was soon laid up with an old trollop. Her fine feathers made me sneeze no end! Soon afterwards I managed to take passage and return home, just down the coast from here. I worked a sloop out of the Yealm for years. Good money but there's too many warships around nowadays. No use being pressed, for our so-called great navy can't best even a Yankee sloop. What's the use of it, then?'

The Royal Navy continued to put pressure on the United States through blockade. From 1813 the British squadron that comprised the North American Station, first under Admiral Borlase Warren and then Rear Admiral Cockburn, patrolled the American coast from Long Island Sound to Pamlico Sound including the Delaware river, Chesapeake Bay and the Albemarle Sound in between.[390] In 1814 Vice Admiral Cochrane took over both the North American and West Indies stations and brought together a

---

388 That acted like a crane.

389 Similar to sentiments written about in *The Wooden World Dissected*, 1802; it was first published in 1760.

390 Some sources spell this as Pamptico.

squadron based on Bermuda and Halifax. They penetrated the Chesapeake and landed troops to burn Washington.[391]

As to Zoilus, being a deserter he had to keep a low profile. With such a long war he lost belief in a good life and, like many others, saw only a dark future. This war had persisted on and off for twenty-one years and had ruined many lives and brought poverty and distress. But he had employment. As to Taunton, he looked at Zoilus and said to himself, *Fool. At least you have never spent time in a French prison; unlike me.*

---

[391] Many American sources afterwards thought him no better than a marauder and buccaneer.

Chapter 7

Rule, Britannia! Rule the Waves

Friday, 2 September 1814

Dear Diary,

I received a letter today from the chairman of the society who has asked me to write an article for the next journal. It will cover recent developments with steam-vessels and innovations that benefit naval yards. I shall begin to gather my notes, all the while digesting news of our new treaty with the Dutch![392] It appears we have retained some West Indies estates, the Cape and some places in the east. This perennial war has at least given us some benefits and the Cape will help our navy immeasurably. I wonder how this affects the slave trade?

Wednesday, 7 September 1814.

Dear Diary,

Having better organised my notes and thoughts I must say I am struck more than ever how Lord Stanhope was correct! I have re-read his 1794 letter with renewed enthusiasm. Like a prophet he stated, even warned us, that 'ships of any size, and for certain reasons the larger the better, may be navigated in any narrow or other sea without sails (though occasionally with), but so as to go without wind, and even directly against both wind and waves... [steam ships would] *shortly render all the existing navies of the world (I mean military navies) no better than lumber.* For what can ships do that are dependent upon the wind and weather against fleets wholly independent of either? Therefore the boasted superiority of the English navy is no more. We must have a new one. The French and other nations will, for the same reasons, have their new ones.'[393]

---

392 The Anglo-Dutch Treaty of 1814, signed 13 August 1814.
393 Preble, 1895, 38.

These sentiments were made twenty years ago. The age of sail must soon pass, as all things eventually do; for British oak will soon be exhausted and steam ships already sail successfully around Britain. The *Naval Chronicle* recently reported the steam-yacht *Thames* to have 'twice crossed St. George's Channel and sailed round Land's End, and is the first steam-vessel that ever traversed these seas.'[394] It is truly a new age. I believe I will start my piece with steam-vessels.

Thursday, 8 September 1814.

Dear Diary,

Everyone knows that the times, fashions and sentiments change; but I wonder if the admiralty realises that the Royal Navy must also change. The French and Americans conduct experiments with steam powered vessels, and the name of Fulton is on all our minds.[395] But we have not been idle. I will write about notable examples of fortitude and experiment and begin my account in 1793 at the commencement of our conflict with France.

I shall mention James Rumsey's steamboat on the Thames (which was able to move against the tide); and John Smith's steamboat on the Duke of Bridgewater Canal. Then Edward Thomason's steam-boat fire-ship of 1796 and the *Charlotte Dundas* back in 1802. Perhaps I will thereafter bridge a few years, with some technical considerations of course, until 1812 when the *Comet* of Glasgow became Europe's first steam vessel for commercial trade. To think how, within a short time, such a thing seems commonplace! I will follow with details of the *Elizabeth* and others.

I wish to stress how the Royal Navy, our wooden wall and senior service, must keep pace or fall behind. If not, Britain and our empire is doomed to become a far lesser power. But just imagine where we would be with a fleet of steam-vessels!

Saturday, 24 September 1814.

Dear Diary,

As I am currently residing in Portsmouth I have revisited the block-mills and I must concur with a recent article in the *Pantologia* that says, 'the blocks... used in the navy are made in Portsmouth by means of circular saws

---

394 *Naval Chronicle*, 1815, 34.

395 An American who pioneered steam powered ships on the Hudson. The man was Robert Fulton.

and other machinery, which have been lately erected by a most ingenious mechanic. This machinery performs the several operations from the rough timber to the perfect block, in the completest manner possible. The whole is worked by means of a steam engine; the manual labour required is simply to supply the wood as it is wanted to the several parts of the machinery, so that the commonest labourer almost may be made to act in this business with very little instruction.'[396] It is as if I had written this piece myself! I will include the marvel of block-mills in my own article.

Should I mention the current fashion for some labourers in the north to make a fuss about such machinery? Yet, what do they signify? Surely, on a national scale only results matter. The new machinery they complain of, in Halifax of all places, produces cloth for the navy. These so-called workers, Luddites I hear them called, must realise how the Royal Navy has to clothe her sailors? Why would they put our men at risk? Heaven forbid if they descend on Portsmouth! The fleets require thousands of pulley blocks every year and the new machines are able to produce them in large numbers. Simple working men cannot understand the necessity of change. Luddites be damned! Transport them all, I say.

What has Fitzgerald written about them? *Who makes the quartern loaf and Luddites rise? Who fills the butchers' shops with large blue flies? Who thought in flames St James's court to pinch? Who burnt the wardrobe of poor Lady Finch? Why he, who, forging for this Isle a yoke, Reminds me of a line I lately spoke, 'The tree of freedom is the British oak.' Bless every man possessed of aught to give; Long may Long Tilney Wellesley Long Pole live; God bless the army, bless their coats of scarlet, God bless the navy, bless the Princess Charlotte.*[397]

The block mills are a marvel! Brunel has done wonders by connecting wheels to their axles on the principle of friction.[398] To see them operate is a wonder.

Sunday, 25 September 1814.

Dear Diary,

An *Analytical Index* of patents granted between 1795 and 1802 gives a detailed series of innovations made for the better manufacture of cordage, another vital element for our sailing ships. It mentions Balfour's means to

---

396 *Pantologia*, 1813, under BLO.
397 *The Edinburgh Review*, 1812, 438.
398 Brewster and Ferguson, 1823, 179.

produce rope and says, 'The effect... to make every yarn employed in the composition of the ropes and cordage, bear its proper and equal proportion of the stress.'[399] There are details of Chapman's patent for making cordage; Mitchell's patent 'for a method of manufacturing cables, hawsers, or shroud-laid ropes, and other cordage, on a scientific principle'; Huddart's patents for an improved method of registering, or forming, the strands in the machinery for manufacturing cordage and improvements with cordage. Any one of them would enhance my article. I must say how impressive it is to pry into any ropeyard and find there the largest cables at one hundred fathoms in length and comprised of more than 3200 yarns! What delightful things we create.

Thursday, 20 October 1814.

Dear Diary,

I have arrived safely in Plymouth after a dismal journey to news of the burning of Washington and bombardment of Fort McHenry, Baltimore.[400] What the world has come to, to abuse our brothers so. Otherwise, I was pleased to meet with an old friend and discuss my article at length. It occasioned me to remember the time back in September 1800 here in Plymouth when I had the good fortune to be present when Robert Seppings raised the *San Josef* by means of his new method. The *Register* wrote a description of it: '...for suspending, instead of lifting, ships, for the purpose of clearing them from their blocks; by which a very great saving will accrue to the public; and also two-thirds of the time formerly used in this operation.'[401] It was a most memorable and emotional event to observe, and although I was not invited to join the celebratory meal afterwards I still enjoyed a wonderful repast at the *George*.

Friday, 21 October 1814.

Dear Diary,

Let us not forget there remains a war to be won, and is there not a continual battle to gain an edge in the manufacture and production of warships and their needs? Our shipwrights and mechanics are as much heroes as any

---

399 *An Analytical Index,*1806, 39.
400 The Royal Navy bombarded the fort 13-14 September 1814.
401 *The Annual Register*, 1807, 870.

Nelson or Byron's *Corsair*.[402] We must remember that! They will give us innovations. We are such an industrious and inventive people.

Our rivals will no doubt pounce upon their ideas as soon as they make them, for the enemy receive intelligence as much as we do in turn about them. What with confounded spies and the telegraph nothing remains hidden for long in this modern age. I'll wager the French are astonished with Plymouth's breakwater. What we can achieve with a will!

Tuesday, 1 November 1814.

Dear Diary,
A momentous day, in Vienna delegates will sit in congress to discuss what will happen when the dust has settled. Europe is not the same as it was in 1803 and so far removed from what it was in 1793 it beggars belief.

And what strange and awful news from London! There has been a great flood of beer![403] On 17 October a vat burst and supposedly more than 3,000 barrels of strong beer poured out and destroyed two houses, filled up local cellars, burst walls asunder, washed a woman out of a window and dashed her to pieces, suffocated a servant and killed eight people. How precious is our time on this mortal plane.

I will conclude my article on the subject of our precious industry, which must be protected. It falls to our navy in the first instance. I foresee a day when we will be fully at peace. What then will be the future for the Navy? What sorts of warships must be built? It is all so obvious! – steam-ships able to carry as large a broadside as any sailing ship. All that remains to achieve this is to convince the Admiralty and the Navy Board.

The American war caused much soul searching in British naval and political circles. Maclay, in his later *History of the United States Navy*, sourced *The Times* which reported in 1812, 'The loss of a single frigate by us, it is true, is but a small one; when viewed as a part of the British navy it is almost nothing; yet under all the circumstances of the two countries to which the vessels belonged, we know not any calamity of twenty times its proportions that might have been attended with more serious consequences to the worsted party.'[404] When another British frigate was lost the same newspaper exclaimed, 'In the name of God, what was done with this immense

---

402 A popular verse tale of 1814.
403 Account given in Urban, 1814, 390.
404 Maclay, 1894, viii.

superiority of force? Oh, what a charm is hereby dissolved! The land spell of the French is broken (at Moscow), and so is our sea spell!'[405]

Initially the Royal Navy struggled to transfer ships to North America, but after February 1813 it was a different story as she began to assert herself on the American littoral with the arrival of Admiral Warren and the 74s *San Domingo* and *Marlborough, Statira* (38), *Maidstone* (36), and the 18s *Fantome* and *Mohawk*.[406] Thereafter, the American war was mostly conducted within her own territory.

On 3 April 1813 the Royal Navy sent a hundred men, in various boats taken off the *San Domingo, Maidstone, Marlborough* and *Statira*, to cut out four schooners found in the Rappahannock river.[407] Her sailors had to row fifteen miles to reach the enemy. Two of the captured schooners later entered the British service.

Thereafter, thanks to the release of troops from Europe and the arrival of Rear Admiral Malcolm with further ships for the station, in 1814 Rear Admiral Cochrane 'penetrated up the Patuxent, the Potomac, and other rivers in Virginia, and inflicted heavy losses on the enemy, who were defeated with the loss of large amounts of military stores. On the 22nd of August the rear-admiral, taking with him the armed boats of the squadron, attacked and dispersed the American Commodore Barney's flotilla of gunboats.'[408] British seamen assisted a small force put ashore that bested the Americans at Bladensburg, entered Washington and burned the White House on 24 August 1814.

The *Seahorse* (38) and *Euryalus* (36), in company with the 8-gun mortar ships *Aetna, Devastation, Erebus* and *Meteor* (and a dispatch boat) took possession of Fort Washington on 28 August 1814 after a bombardment. Captain Gordon's later letter[409] to Cochrane detailed how this flotilla proceeded up the 'Potowmac'. With no pilots they had to proceed with caution, with 'the severest labour', but grounded multiple times and 'were employed, warping, for five whole successive days, with the exception of a few hours, a distance of more than fifty miles.'

A joint land and sea attack was made against Baltimore in September 1814. Fort McHenry guarded the entrance to the city with a bar 'running

---

405 *Ibid.*
406 Low, 1872, 418.
407 James reported these to be the *Dolphin* (12), *Arab* (7), and the 6s *Lynx* and *Racer*. James, 1817, 368.
408 Low, *ibid,* 422.
409 Taken from James, 1817, cxliv to cxlix.

across the harbour, on which there are only about fourteen or fifteen feet of water'.[410] On 11 September a squadron under Cochrane in the *Royal Oak* (74) anchored near North Point south east of the city and landed regular troops, 600 seamen and marines. The *Severn* (38); the 36s *Euryalus*, *Havannah* and *Hebrus*; the rocket-ship *Erebus* (18); and the mortar-ships *Aetna*, *Devastation*, *Meteor*, *Terror* and *Volcano* were sent against the fort. The land battle which followed resulted in the loss to the British of one 'clerk, five seamen, and one marine killed',[411] with three officers, thirty seamen and fifteen marines wounded. As to the squadron, several vessels grounded but the mortar and rocket ships managed to bombard the fort. A diversion made by boats' crews at night came to nothing and the squadron soon departed to re-embark land troops and sail off.

The British gained some successes but no one could deny the Americans had their own share of victories. They had a clear superiority in warship construction, effective gunnery and excellent seamanship which told anyone who paid attention that there was a need for the Royal Navy to innovate and not simply crush the enemy by sheer numbers. Maclay later considered that 'from the very beginning the American navy became noted for new ideas and innovations which revolutionized old theories, and brought about entirely new methods and results in naval warfare. The English were compelled to accept these new ideas despite their own obstinacy.'[412]

Maclay noted that in the war against France the Royal Navy suffered five defeats in two hundred conflicts, but against America suffered 'fifteen severe defeats' out of eighteen engagements. In the War of 1812 British sea commerce, and the minds of British subjects, were disturbed; this was similar to the previous American war when 'The complete reversal of results which followed a trial of strength and skill with the Americans produced in Englishmen a kind of stupor.'[413]

After so many years of war there was deep sense of weariness in Britain. American and French prizes delighted, yet embarrassed. So far as Britain's senior service was concerned four glimmers of light punctured the gloom: two broad and two narrow. The two broad were with how the 'industrial revolution' had propelled British industry beyond that of any other power; the second was the wealth the country commanded, which enabled her to

---

410 Allen, 1852, 483.

411 *Ibid.*

412 From a piece about Maclay's *A History of the United States Navy* in *School*, 1884, 149. The sentiment fits.

413 *Scientific American*, 1894, 230.

put to sea such colossal fleets. The two narrower glimmers of hope were the entrepreneurial spirit of the nation, and the new spirit of enterprise that slowly overturned inaction within the naval administration.

Certain ideas and innovations then introduced to the Navy helped improve the support of the fleets and their warships. It might have been expected that such ideas would have been home grown, as there was a 'feeling of repugnance to everything French, and indeed that suspicion and jealousy with which everything foreign was regarded, attained in England an intensity... greater perhaps than at any other [time] on record';[414] yet it was a Frenchman who most helped usher in mass production to the Navy. Marc Isambard Brunel arrived in England in 1799, married Plymouth-born Sophia Kingdom (who had strong naval connections), and in 1801 patented machinery to better manufacture naval blocks. He caught the attention of the admiralty.

Up until Brunel's patent, blocks for the navy had been produced at high cost with little standardised finish. Samuel Taylor partly held the contract to provide them, and he wrote a letter, dated 5 March 1801, in which he laid out the method of production. Two to five loads of timber were placed by a machine under a saw and cut to length, removed to another saw where they were shaped, and 'mortises... cut in by hand, which wholly completes the block, except with a broad chisel cutting out the roughness of the teeth of the saw, and the scores for the strapping of the rope.'[415] Taylor was convinced this system could not be improved, and the naval administration enabled him to keep the contract for years.

Blocks and pulleys, as part of running rigging, were mainstays of sailing ships and vessels, and although vital for the raising and lowering of yards they were cumbersome. The term 'block' for sailors referred to a piece of wood in which 'the shivers of pullies are placed, and wherein the running-ropes go'.[416] Some were single blocks, others double with up to five shivers contained within.

In 1807 Thomas Young wrote, 'Pullies, and their combinations in blocks, are universally employed on board of ships. They are very convenient where only a moderate increase of power is required; but in order to procure a very great advantage, the number of separate pullies or sheathes must be very much multiplied; a great length of rope must also be employed; and it is

---

414 Beamish, 1862, 43.
415 Beamish, *ibid,* 51.
416 *Encyclopaedia Britannica*, 1797, 307.

said that in a pair of blocks with five pullies in each, two thirds of the force are lost by friction and the rigidity of the ropes.'[417]

A new British naval spirit commenced well before the War of 1812. Samuel Bentham was made Inspector-General of Naval Works in 1796, and his widowed wife later wrote how he introduced numerous small alterations that added up to a great weight of improvement. He dealt with fraud and abuses, naval architecture (the way warships are designed), engineering, management of the yards and their mechanical and ordnance aspects. He considered warships weak and constructed at too high a cost. By way of example he had built, to his own designs, the 24-gun sloops *Arrow* and *Dart*; the *Millbrook* (16); and the 12s *Eling*, *Nelly* and *Redbridge*. They were longer than other similar types and 'raked forward like a Thames wherry… better supported when pitching and rolling in a sea, than others where the sides retire inwards above the water-line.'[418] He also innovated the way their timbers were cut and laid so as to lower 'deadwood' weight, ideas that preceded similar improvements made by Robert Seppings. According to his wife he effectively made *'water-tight compartments';*[419] and the height between decks was increased for the crew's comfort and improvement of ventilation and health. Drinking water was contained in metallic tanks, to increase the amount carried and preserve it longer, which allowed his ships to remain at sea for longer. At Portsmouth, he replaced jetties and basins so that 'Portsmouth dockyard was… rendered pre-eminently suited… for the most important business of that port in times of war, namely, the *graving* of ships of the line; that is, examining their bottoms and executing trifling repairs to them.'[420]

Perhaps Bentham's true gift was to perceive small abuses of time and materials. For instance, time lost when artificers had to row back and forth to warships at moorings to conduct repairs; and how, with so many materials rowed out to warships often at distance and in crowded waters, many items went missing. He made it that within the bounds of Portsmouth dockyard up to 'twelve ships of the line, besides smaller vessels, could be repaired, fitted, and stored'[421] and better supervised.

Steam engines were introduced to dockyards in 1798 and the first block mills built at Portsmouth in 1803. Bentham's wife argued that her husband

---

417 Young, 1807, 206/7.
418 Bentham, 1862, 107.
419 *Ibid,* 110. Her italics.
420 Bentham, *ibid*, 104.
421 *Ibid,* 105.

made designs for steam-powered machines to make naval blocks; that in a letter dated 1 June 1802 he had written, 'these engines should be set up in Plymouth dockyard immediately, to be worked by the steam-engine.'[422]

Bentham was also involved with improvements to the naval yard at Dock. He considered her landing jetties, inaccessible at low tide, to be inadequate and so proposed a boat harbour. Storehouses there had very high ceilings, so he had them fitted out to take a further floor and increase the amount of stores contained within.

The senior service also benefited from improvements in the way work was done within her yards. After 1803 'the advantages of task and job-work began to be appreciated.'[423] So large had the Royal Navy become that repair, refit and replenishment of her warships was a labour of Herculean proportions. Dockyard employees often had to work seven days a week to keep pace, and even then struggled to keep up. Apprentices to shipwrights were mostly 'youths who had received a better education than those who were bound to the labouring mechanics of the dockyards',[424] but due to a long war this had become less the case. There were no official means to instruct apprentices in the theory of ship-building until 1811 when a college to educate them was opened at Portsmouth. The School of Naval Architecture soon showed positive results. Slowly, the age-old reliance on 'knowledge' and 'experience' over 'science' diminished.

It took years to fully comprehend the extent of innovation which took place during these latter years of the war, but there were clear signs of change at the time. Steam-vessels were one such marker. In 1796 Earl Stanhope had corresponded with the Lords of the Admiralty on the matter, and they had sanctioned his experiments. So sure was he of successfully placing a steam-vessel on the Thames, one that would actually work, he had signed a bond 'dated June 30, 1794, with a penalty to himself of 9000*l*'.[425] He then built what he called an 'Ambi-Navigator ship', the *Kent*. He admitted it took longer to build than he had wished, and he had to ask for an extension of time to prove the vessel. Evan Nepean of the admiralty was not impressed with the results and the 'First Lord of the Admiralty… looked down upon the project as an empty dream.'[426]

---

422 *Ibid,* 224.
423 Fincham, 1851, 145.
424 Fincham, *ibid*, 174.
425 Turnor, 1865, 476.
426 *Ibid.*

However, in 1802 the *Charlotte Dundas* demonstrated the practical use of a steam-vessel by towing two loaded sloops, 'each of seventy tons, a distance of 19½ miles in six hours against a head-wind'.[427] This was revolutionary so far as navigation was concerned, one that Charles MacFarlane considered *the* most important. If there had been a prolonged peace it might have promoted further developments, but war returned and no steam-vessel could then carry an effective broadside. The navy also considered steam vessels unreliable.

For this long war naval funds were for sailing ships. In 1813 the 'sum voted for the ordinary estimate of the navy... was 1,757,928*l*'[428] which did not include sums voted for the extraordinary estimate. Monies were set aside for the alteration of certain warships to strengthen them in line with American frigates but sailing warships remained the only option for the Royal Navy. Nevertheless there occurred a sea-change, albeit one delayed by the necessity of war and the early days of development. It was perceived that however uncertain, steam-navigation had to be considered something for the future.

For ordinary people, wages continued to fall and poverty widened. Between 1811 and 1821 rural population declined,[429] which followed the 'disastrous step... taken... [with] the passing of the Combination Acts. The Act of 1799, which inflicted a new and very serious grievance on the artisan classes, appears to have been rushed through the House of Commons under the influence of a panic... the Combination Act was directed against any seditious conspiracies which might conceal themselves under the form of Trade Societies.'[430] A direct result of the stress of war and fear of invasion was that any secret society was looked upon with deep suspicion, and open debates that criticised the king or government were deemed seditious. Whereas Luddites came to be associated with wilful destruction – '*destroy the machine that ate his bread*'[431] – in truth they were concerned with poverty, wages and working conditions. King Ludd was a myth, based upon a disgruntled Leicestershire worker of the 1770s who broke his 'machine' in a fit of pique.

Halifax was a centre of the cloth trade as was 'the vale of Ripponden, whence [came] a large portion of the cloth used for clothing the British

---

427 MacFarlane, 1861, 441.
428 As of 2019 this was equivalent to some £12 billion.
429 According to Toynbee from 35 percent to 33 percent. Toynbee, 1887, 88.
430 *The Economic Review,* 1894, 12.
431 Cowgill, 1862, iv.

navy'.[432] The long war years after 1793 helped expand this industry, 'as to excite the jealousy of the Leeds merchants, who had been previously used to buy the same articles from the lower manufacturers at their cloth hall, and parliament was petitioned, in 1794 and 1806, to prevent any merchant from becoming a manufacturer.' There was uncertainty, and a whole region said to have employed a 'great number of hands' became unsettled. Disturbance spread, caused alarm, and some within the naval administration must have worried over supplies of cloth for the fleets.

In his maiden speech to Parliament on 27 February 1812 Lord Byron stood to defend the workers of the nation after a bill had been proposed to make 'frame-breaking'[433] a crime. He said, 'During a short time I recently passed in Nottingham, not twelve hours elapsed without some fresh act of violence... they have arisen from circumstances of the most unparalleled distress... nothing but absolute want could have driven a large and once honest and industrious body of the people into the mission of excesses so hazardous to themselves, their families, and the community... . By the adoption of one species of frame in particular, one man performed the work of many, and the superfluous labourers were thrown out of employment... . The rejected workmen... conceived themselves to be sacrificed to improvements in mechanism... can we forget that it is the bitter policy, the destructive warfare of the last eighteen years, which has destroyed their comfort, your comfort, all men's comfort?'[434]

Byron stated that people, in stations not far below that of the lords in parliament, now suffered a world of bankruptcy, fraud and felony; and with the need for military forces to guard against mischief, both foreign and domestic, 'the country suffers from the double infliction of an idle military and a starving population.'[435] *What was it,* he argued, *to take cities abroad if at home the militia must be let loose on British citizens? That the mob must be so abused?* 'It is the mob that labour in your fields and serve in your houses, that man your navy, and recruit your army, that have enabled you to defy all the world.'[436]

Perhaps Byron's most stinging criticism was when he said, 'I have traversed the seat of war in the peninsula, I have been in some of the most oppressed provinces of Turkey, but never under the most despotic of infidel

---

432 *A Dictionary, geographical, statistical, and historical,* 1854, 951.
433 The destruction of cotton-making machinery.
434 *Cobbett's Parliamentary Debates Vol XXI,* 1812, 965-7.
435 *Ibid.*
436 *Ibid.*

governments did I behold such squalid wretchedness as I have seen since my return.'

In 1814 a Plymouth widow enjoyed two festive events: the wedding of her younger sister (one of hundreds of marriages the city registered during each year of the war[437]) and the return from foreign service of the 93rd Highlanders. On the subject of her sister she had mixed feelings. She herself had married young and at 29 years of age might have done so again but she could not face the prospect of losing another husband. The one she had had been a marine captain who sailed off to war a week after they exchanged their wedding vows. She was so deeply in love she thought her heart might burst with the separation. Two months later he returned home terribly mangled, delirious and not long for this world.

The wedding of her sister made her think back to when her husband lay dying in the Royal Hospital at Stonehouse. Her mind had been consumed with regret and dark thoughts on the futility of war. She had visited him every day, although he seemed not to recognise her. At the time a commotion broke out over findings of the naval inspection into fraud and abuses at the hospital. Some nurses gossiped openly about waste of stores, the terrible state of the hospital cellar and storerooms, and how they might no longer be allowed to take hospital linen for their own use.[438] A bizarre quantity of porter had been found to have been consumed in the hospital, some 4,000 gallons over a period of six months, likewise an inordinate amount of wine, fruit and eggs.[439] She thought it deplorable how dozens of surly labourers seemed to have had the run of the place.

She was upset but put it down to her being pregnant. She made her husband as comfortable as possible and mourned his inevitable death. After the funeral her senses dulled to oblivion, but she had a baby to deliver and at least had a dowry, a wealthy family and a widow's pension[440] to keep her comfortable. If she had wanted to she could have read *The Annual Register* which reported the pensions given out by the navy for that year: For widows

---

437 *The Annual Register*, 1802, 240. 'During a war, about 400 marriages are celebrated annually at Plymouth and in the vicinity, between the seamen of the royal navy and the women who receive them on shore.'

438 *Cobbett's Parliamentary Debates*, 1805, 1087. It was reported that this 'practice had subsisted many years… the use of linen, tunnery wares, and other articles the property of the public'.

439 *Cobbett's Parliamentary Debates,* ibid.

440 *The Annual Register of 1808,* 241.

of 'officers of marines, and of subalterns of the navy – 1,852' from a total of £62,884.

After the birth of her girl the widow returned to her paints. Patriotic seascapes were her forte, large romantic canvases of ships at anchor and at sea, and she sold more than was put in storage. Her own style showed ships at a distance – she found it easier to be vague with the details – and her favourite place to set up her easel was at Jennycliff for the fine views of the Sound, Drake's Island and the wonder of the breakwater under construction. She adored Sir Joshua Reynolds, a Plympton man, for his style; Joshua Cristall, for his watercolours; and Samuel Atkins for his renditions of warships.

She was often seen trudging along the back lanes with a pack, walking stick, umbrella, her delightful girl and nursemaid in tow. A well-read woman, she was short-sighted, had a wicked sense of humour and a dusky voice that put men in a spin. Seldom was she alone on her trips for there was always some naval or military man intent on providing her company and assistance. Although she flirted she knew how to keep them at a distance. Never did she cause a scene, nor promote gossip against her. She had her husband's memory and her reputation to think about.

In January 1814 her daughter turned eleven and suddenly became curious to a fault. The raven-haired lass wanted to know about her father, the Royal Marines, her aunt's wedding and boys. One day, as more than twenty inches of snow fell outside their windows,[441] her mother answered all her questions except those about boys, for 'There are some things a lady does not talk about.'

'But, mother, they are all so… strange.'

'Believe me dear, it is why they go to war so much.'

The widow and her daughter were part of a sheltered human archipelago set amidst a wide and destitute country. Patriotism and fortitude swelled her heart to the point she struggled to admit how the army and navy, so desperate for men, robbed the gallows of some of its victims.[442] Beyond Plymouth, far into the interior, whole towns had been swept clean of those who often saw drunkenness as a virtue, swearing that to kill the enemy was an honour. She and her community considered every one of them a darling hero who stood up to wicked Boney. As to the poor and starving of Plymouth, East Stonehouse and Dock, she blithely ignored them; but

---

441 *Annual Register,* 1815, 5.

442 Ned Ward uses a similar phrase: 'and the Army and the Navy robbing the Gallows of the rest'. Ward, 1756, 71.

whenever a subscription was set afoot it was fashionable to respond with charity. After handfuls of impoverished Spanish women and children arrived in a terrible state of wretchedness[443] she gave away two dresses, a shawl, a bonnet and her daughter's old clothes. She never left the house to do so; instead she gave them to her maid to deliver. She might have ventured out if they had been American prisoners – for she considered them cousins – or if they had been French – for there was much to admire about France – but Spaniards were far too foreign for her.

Before the wedding it became known that Bonaparte's Continental System had collapsed.[444] Her father, a man of fixed habits, always expected his family to be together on Sundays. Which meant his wife, two sons, reluctant daughters and grandchildren all convened en masse. When the May weather was glorious they were joined by their future in-law. Over a less than adequate roast beef the host made his guest tell them what the Continental System had meant. The poor man did not know but still spent half an hour trying to impress. The widow looked over her glasses, sighed inwardly and tried to interject about how some countries, Russia for example, avoided it for risk of permanent ruin to their gentry.[445] But no older man at the table would listen to a woman converse upon politics, however superior her knowledge. Her younger brother sniggered at her obvious annoyance, received a kick under the table for his pains, and in retaliation asked his father to tell them of his time in Italy – *What, when I did the tour? Yes, father. All of it* – and smirked as his sister let out a stifled moan. The meal was nearly ruined when her daughter noticed and asked, *Mother why are you angry?* A bright moment of her day was when she presented a large painting as a wedding gift. Her future brother-in-law cared little for it but her sister was delighted.

The widow was concerned what would happen to Britain when war ended. What of those industries which supported the colossal fleets? What of men thrown on the beach? For the war would have to end one day and her sister's betrothed owned a small business that might suffer. As it turned out, two days after her sister's wedding the Highlanders were to parade through town, so there was much to look forward to and keep her mind off those worries.

One languid afternoon, as her red outfit for the wedding was completed, her daughter asked about the ensemble. 'Mother, why the blue cuffs?'

---

443 *The Annual Register,* ibid, 3.
444 It ended by April 1814.
445 *The Popular Encyclopaedia*, 1817, 421.

As her maid adjusted pins and material the widow replied, 'I have designed it in memory of your father.'

The girl continued to dress her doll and went quiet, but was soon asking questions again. 'You said father's uniform changed?'

'Yes, dear, at the peace. But the navy has changed too. Their ships might look the same but their men appear differently now. Naval officers have taken to wearing their hats fore and aft. I was your age when I first saw an epaulette. You can't move for them now; and whatever happened to the wig I cannot say. Imagine what the navy will be like when you're my age!'

On the topic of male fashion she hoped to avoid any mention of the tight fitting pantaloons that some men favoured. They were far too revealing for her modesty and some carried so much weight they made themselves look ridiculous. She secretly hoped her future brother-in-law would be more circumspect with his wedding outfit. His hams were massive.

'Mother, will the Americans invade?'

'Worry not, dear, we seem to be giving them what for. We burned their President's house, didn't we? The navy is our front line of defence, although not the only one. The enemy risk much if they try to land here. The garrison would see to that. Now, what do you think? Do I look like a marine?'

The widow apprehended something of national and foreign politics but was unconcerned regarding local issues. However, when her daughter pointed out beggars in the street, she began to take notice. One injured and homeless man she came across wore a faded marine jacket. She hoped he had stolen it but what if he had not? She did not like the probable answer. Britain had had many fine naval and military successes, but at what cost?

One day she found herself alone in her parlour and for the first time she began to wonder about her possessions. On her mantle, and dotted around her rooms, were items of value. Some had been wedding gifts but most had been purchased in the years after. Did she really need the Hepplewhite? Was the Chippendale cabinet necessary? Perhaps so, when she considered what they meant for the country. Britain manufactured goods to sell at home and abroad, and British businesses shipped and sold them in foreign markets. Merchantmen were protected by British warships and they brought home many foreign goods. It was the power and majesty of the British merchant and naval fleets that guaranteed and encouraged British exports and imports. Her own family had certainly benefited. Perhaps then, to own valuable things was a proper thing to do. Perhaps, she thought, it was patriotic.

What else had been affected by the Royal Navy? Language certainly, even fashions. Her husband had felt pride for both his uniform and service. He had often strolled through town to be seen. It was all the thing and the number of military and naval uniforms on the streets was remarkable. The constant babblement of soldiers, marines and sailors had taught her to use many of their nautical phrases in normal speech. She often heard people say they were 'taken aback', or female friends gossip about how so and so was or was not 'above board'. Her brother once said that a cutting remark 'took the wind out of my sails'. She thought herself in 'close quarters' with her family and struggled to 'fathom'[446] most of them. At the 'bitter end' of the war there might be the 'devil to pay'.

On the day of the wedding her daughter couldn't keep still. She ran through the house, upset the maid, made the dog bark and spilled milk on her dress. Their route to the church took them to the coast with fine views towards Cornwall. They saw a squadron of warships in the offing which reminded them the country was still at war. The girl looked out of the carriage window and said, 'Mother, is one of those ships the one father served on?'

The widow held her daughter close and looked outside. 'I don't know, dear. They all look the same to me. But there are an awful lot of them. It looks like they are off somewhere. America, perhaps?'

The wedding turned out to be splendid enough, but all too brief. Her sister looked beautiful, her brother-in-law fashionable and the men did not get too drunk.

As the wedding bliss faded the town became excited by a military parade. As the 93rd Highlanders marched past she was tempted to shield her daughter's eyes from the sight of so many kilted men with bare legs.[447] When someone in the crowd said they had been at the Cape since 1805, she started to cry. A lone tear at first then full floods streamed down her cheeks. Like everyone else she was heartily sick of the war, of the death of so many sailors, soldiers and marines. She reckoned that only a few in the hundreds gathered in that crowd would *not* have been affected by such loss. The highlanders had been absent for almost ten years! How many thousands more like them had been cast abroad? Sailors perpetually on blockade off some godforsaken foreign port. How many had never returned home?

Her daughter realised her mother was crying. So too was every other woman present and even some men had to wipe moisture from their eyes.

---

446 *The Lady's Magazine*, 1782, 532. This had long been in popular use.
447 Walker, 1890, 78. The 'men were of the most stalwart proportions'.

The girl asked her mother how long the soldiers would be home, but she only received a firm squeeze of her hand.

Normality, as it was, returned. At the next concert held in the Long Room, late for the season but supported in a most splendid manner, the widow was accompanied by her brothers, father and some of his business acquaintances. Boors every one of them, who as soon as they met two naval officers set to drinking seven bottles of wine. *Let's bowse up the jib*,[448] they said. She gave a sigh, for it was what Ned Ward once wrote about the British being a community of continuous tippling, nightly suck-bottle dining, overt inebrious health drinking, tittle-tattle and promotion of swill-bellied sops.[449] Yet she forgave the naval officers for they deserved to live a life, for who knew when it would be taken from them? She managed to get her older brother to take her home and was thankful to depart a room made as mad as an asylum for lunatics and idiots.[450]

The winter of 1814/15 proved severe and much colder than the previous one. The widow enjoyed reading about the Thames Frost Fair and the snows fell and fell. From her bedroom window she saw Dartmoor covered in white. As Christmas neared, a frightful storm hit the Channel. The winds buffeted her windows making the house moan. She dreaded to think what it must be like at sea, red raw hands on cold ropes, fearful of a rogue wave or a lee shore. The next morning she found trees upturned, branches scattered and leaves blown akimbo so she was not surprised to hear how shipping had been thrown into confusion.[451] Some ships at anchor in the Cattewater had broken their cables, despite the breakwater, and a whole fleet of merchantmen limped in over successive days.

Confined within her warm home she took to reading Debrett's peerage for any mention of naval or marine persons of note. *Baron Glenbervie, late chief secretary in Ireland then representative in parliament for Irish Town then Fowey then Midhurst then Plympton and then Hastings. Appointed governor of Cape of Good Hope in 1800; kissed his majesty's hand in 1801; pay-master general of the forces.* Oh, my! She liked the armorial plates, and when she saw *died without issue* she looked to her daughter; at least that had not been the case with her father.

---

448 Smyth, 1867, 125, 'a colloquialism to denote the act of tippling: it is an old phrase... from the Dutch *buyzen*, to booze.'

449 Ward, 1756, 1.

450 A common phrase at the time.

451 *Annual Register,* 1815, 111.

March 1815 continued with cold and blustery weather. One dreary day a noise was heard outside the house as a man came to the door. She made her daughter sit down and they both waited until the maid knocked and entered. *A man to see you, miss.* It turned out to be a kind old friend of her father who seemed terribly upset.

'Whatever is the matter?' she asked.

The man was apoplectic. 'Can you fathom it, my dear? Although an outlaw, he's landed in France!'

Confused she asked, 'Who, prey tell?'

The old man coughed and blurted out, 'Napoléon. Old Boney is back!'

Chapter 8

All their Attempts to Bend thee Down

He had grown up in Madras, the ward of a strict Company man, so had run away to sea as soon as possible. With less than one year on a sluggish transport he could not claim to have any great experience, nor any knowledge of battle, but he could see that the complement of his new ship was bad. The *Penguin* was fine enough, less than two years old, but seventeen of her crew were boys; many of the older men had previously been discharged and most of the younger lot pressed into service. Only a dozen or so had ever been in action, and here they were alone in the middle of the southern Atlantic chasing a strange sail which was certainly not the ship they were after.[452] Few seemed of good humour.[453]

After being paid off at the Cape he had found himself in need of employment so had joined the *Penguin* together with twelve Royal Marines loaned off the *Medway* (74), for the ship had suffered from sickness. He found her officers to be competent but almost everyone else dangerous murkhs.[454] He worried how the ship was worked, and tried not to think about the dregs who served the guns. In their hands the ordnance might as well be firecrackers. He could only conclude that the situation in England, as to the supply of men, must be truly pitiful to have put such a crew to sea.

With a lowly position in the hierarchy of the ship he had no idea as to their heading nor position. Even if informed he would have understood little. He pulled ropes, that was all. It was enough to know the sun was out, the wind fresh and the monstrous cliffs of a triangular cloud-clad island four miles behind them. He heard the master call that island Tristan da Cunha. He sensed their captain was cautious in his approach of the strange sail.[455] They were now at range.

---

452 The US privateer *Young Wasp*. See Roosevelt, 1882, 168.
453 James, 1836, 384.
454 'Murkh' is a Panjabi word for fool.
455 The *Hornet's* captain thought so in his autobiography: Biddle, 1883, 399.

Standing on deck he heard the ship's ensign snapping and flapping above as one of their guns went off. All eyes looked ahead to see how the strange sail reacted. When it luffed and hoisted colours there was an audible gasp. An old idler whispered, 'American, by God!'

As the *Penguin* turned to offer her broadside the enemy ship's side suddenly went white with smoke. He heard the boom as the shock of hot metal hit them. Then, confused moments, before they returned a ragged and none too convincing salvo. To the sound of grunts and muffled curses the engagement began.

Because of tales he had heard and read he assumed this would be another British success at sea. One where the skill and fortitude of those on board united to bring victory and where everyone knew their place.

For no reason he could think of the daylight suddenly seemed brighter. Noises sounded louder and his inner feelings became more distinct. It was as though Kali[456] had intervened to cause time to stutter. He was young and never once thought he could die.

At first he thought the American ship – he heard the name *Hornet* – had chosen to run, but she only moved to a safer distance to play the *Penguin* with frightfully effective gunnery. Within minutes their rigging was shot to pieces and the hull and men battered. Those who stood near the captain, including himself, gritted their teeth when they heard him say, *We cannot stand this! We must run her aboard.*[457]

He knew this sorry lot of men and boys would struggle to do that. He made ready to board nonetheless as the *Penguin* made for the American. They managed to run inboard between the enemy's main and mizzen masts. The shock of impact shivered everything and everyone. It seemed they rode a horse over a fence for they rose up and up, taken further by the swell, as wood splintered and rigging fell from above. But the gap between them could not be closed and the American continued to batter them cruelly.

Ready to make the jump he felt calm. Enemy muskets peppered the crew and many fell. One man, a rough squint-eyed fellow he disliked, fell down dead with a smile on his face. He looked at him with amazement. Was he happy to die?

A loud commotion got his attention. He turned to see their captain also lay dead! He sensed the resolve of others turn to slush. Men stood

---

456 Hindu goddess of time and death.
457 Biddle, *ibid.*

dumbfounded. What should they do? It was a relief when Lieutenant McDonald took command.

There followed a sudden and strange silence, and from the stern of the enemy ship a voice asked them, *Have you surrendered?* It was the Yankee captain. He wondered whether they had; but two of the loaned marines raised their muskets and fired almost point blank at the American captain. One bullet nicked him in the neck, but he stayed standing. In return bullets flew into the two marines, who fell down on deck with heavy thuds. An awful tense momentary pause signified that all lay in the balance. The American captain, his face stern and grave, gave an order to wear and make another broadside.

As the American ship started to move the *Penguin*'s bowsprit fell away. Looking to the guns it was obvious most had been dismounted and few men stood to work them. That decided it. The British colours were lowered. A morose hush descended on deck and British faces lost their vitality. He was startled to hear the engagement had lasted less than half an hour.

Kali's conception of normal time resumed. So badly mauled was the *Penguin* that even he could see the Americans would struggle to take her a prize. For the rest of his life he wondered whether they had conducted themselves well.

Days later he and fellow prisoners were informed they had been captured long after the War of 1812 had ceased. He was freed, sailed to Plymouth, and was paid off. He tried to gain passage back to India, failed, and disappeared. Within a few weeks he was forgotten, a mere name on a muster book.

According to William James, HMS *Penguin* (16) ought to have been tasked to escort a convoy in the English Channel instead of being sent to the Cape of Good Hope. But at the time there had been a sense of urgency that had to be addressed. 'Out of a crew... of 105 men and 17 boys, the Penguin lost her commander, boatswain, and four seamen and marines killed, four others mortally wounded, and her second lieutenant... one master's mate..., one midshipman..., purser's clerk, and 24 seamen and marines wounded, for the most part slightly.'[458]

The *Penguin* first put to sea in September 1814 and was taken on 23 March 1815, long after the treaty that ended the War of 1812 but news had not reached abroad.[459] The USS *Hornet* was off Tristan da Cunha en route

---

458 James, 1836, 385.
459 James reckoned Captain Biddle found out before the engagement, from a neutral. Page 383.

to the East Indies. Archibald Alison wrote that 'long after peace had been signed, the Hornet met the Penguin.... . Both vessels were of equal size and weight of metal, but the American had the advantage in the number and composition of her crew; and after a desperate conflict, in the course of which the brave Captain Dickinson was slain in the very act of attempting to board, the British vessel surrendered, having lost a third of her crew, killed and wounded.'[460] Theodore Roosevelt considered the *Hornet* caused 'fourfold the loss and tenfold the damage she suffered. Hardly any action of the war reflected greater credit than this.'[461]

Despite the absence of large naval battles the final years of the war had the usual run of naval affairs. On 29 January 1813 the Adriatic island of Augusta, or Lastovo, 'surrendered to a British force, consisting of the 38-gun frigate Apollo... Esperanza privateer, and four gun-boats, and 250 troops.'[462] And on 7 February 1813 the *Amelia* (38) fought a long and wicked duel with the *Aréthuse* (40) with shocking loss of life on both sides.

Officers continued to receive recognition. The *London Gazette* mentioned Lieutenant O'Brien who, on 6 January 1813, with boats of the *Bacchante* (38) and *Weasel* (18), captured five gun-boats near Otranto in southern Italy;[463] Lieutenant Devon of the *Blazer* (14) who captured, on 21 March 1813, two Danish boats in the Elbe; Lieutenant Dance of the *Orpheus* (36) who captured, on 28 April 1813, a Danish 'letter of marque'; Captain Lawrence and Lieutenant Westphal who took part in the destruction of a fort and cannon foundry at Havre de Grâce; Lieutenant Shaw who commanded boats off the *Repulse* (74), *Volontaire* (40), *Undaunted* (38) and *Redwing* (18) to blow up a battery and capture six vessels.

The steady accumulation of small but frantic engagements, cutting outs and landings added up so that according to an abstract printed by Joseph Allen, the 'Losses of Line-of Battle Ships and Frigates sustained by the French, Dutch, Spanish, Danish, Russian, Turkish, and American Navies in the War commencing in May, 1803, and ending in July, 1815,'[464] amounted to 55 ships of the line and 79 frigates. Ships and vessels added to the British navy came to 101 of which France suffered the most losses at 59. In the same period the Royal Navy lost no ships of the line but did lose

---

460 Alison, 1841, 347.
461 Roosevelt, *ibid*, 171.
462 Allen,1852, 417.
463 A compendium of the *London Gazette*, later printed in 1849, also mentioned this on
     page 247. All other examples of 1813 from this source.
464 Allen, *ibid*, 502.

eighty-three frigates. Her major losses were due to misfortune, with 161 ships and vessels lost by wreck, 50 by foundering and 3 by fire.

With an eye cast across a greater period of time, from 1793 to 1815, the French suffered the loss of 87 ships of the line, 217 frigates and 408 corvettes – numbers that dwarf the losses incurred by the Spanish and the Dutch. The British lost 7 line of battleships and 27 frigates in battle.[465]

What enabled success in naval battles was in large measure the manoeuvres made by ships and fleets. Père Hoste, a French professor of mathematics, wrote *L'art des armées navales* as early as 1697.[466] It was 'an elementary and distinct exposition of the ordinary manoeuvres at sea, and has no pretensions to any thing more... [and was] highly regarded at the time.' From then until the end of the age of sail a number of books and essays on naval tactics were published. Robert Park's *The Art of Seafighting*[467] was issued in 1706 (mostly written for commanders of merchantmen) that laid out topics such as *The Conduct to be used in Chasing, Shewing how a Ship must be prepared for a Close Fight, Being an Epitomy of the Art of Gunnery and Defensive Fighting in General.* Park wrote his book for, 'Notwithstanding the Usefulness of such a Treatise, yet the Two last Dutch Wars, nor the late long French War produced nothing of this Subject... but what was wrote in the latter part of Queen Elizabeth's Reign, and the beginning of King Charles the First, and 'tis notoriously known Shipping has been almost new modell'd since then.'[468] A full century later, sailors might still have appreciated how Park argued for the way 'Bulkheads... Doors, Look-holes, Ports and Scuttles' were to be ordered in battle, running rigging 'commanded in Close-quarters',[469] and that a gunner's 'Moral Qualifications' required sobriety and vigilance with a need for continual practice of small arms and 'cannon'. Park offered little on movements a warship should make in a sea-fight, only suggestions of ways merchantmen might avoid an enemy, however he did state a truism: 'To clap Ships together without Consideration, belongs rather to a Mad-man than a Man of War.'[470]

In 1762 Christopher O'Bryen used Hoste's book as an extraction for his own work. He argued that admirals had to have 'proper knowledge'

---

465 Data supplied by Lieutenant Nicolas, as found in Allen, *ibid*.
466 Hoste, 1697.
467 Park, 1706, iii
468 *Ibid*, Preface.
469 *Ibid,* 35.
470 *Ibid*, 4.

when 'opposing the enemy, cutting them off, doubling upon, avoiding, or chacing them to the greatest advantage: for all these things require, that an admiral should move each part of his fleet, as the mind moves the different members of the human body.'[471] In other words, similar to chess although movement at sea could so easily become deranged by wind and weather to a point where ships collided or lost the 'favourable opportunity of gaining to windward of, or doubling upon the enemy, which they will undoubtedly avail themselves of'.[472] O'Bryen was of the firm conviction that 'proper' knowledge would rid a commander of such embarrassments.

The main point with line of battleships was to maintain discipline of line, follow signals and be quick to adapt to the situation. 'When a fleet sails before the wind, it has likewise its particular form of sailing, as it has also when it chaces the enemy, makes a retreat, guards a streight or passage, or, is obliged to force through one; or whether at anchor in a road or harbour, or going into either, to insult or attack an enemy.'[473] In effect a naval commander had to take into consideration the best possible form, or evolution, his ships must assume: an approach of an enemy, a retreat, in aid to friendly ships, and maintenance of communication. O'Bryen offered examples for a chase and in line of battle, advantages and disadvantages of being to windward or leeward of an enemy, the importance of the size of line ships in respect of guns they carried and their strength of timber to 'better resist the shot of the enemy',[474] the order of retreat, the form a fleet should sail in and other considerations. Titles of his 'parts' sum up the variables that had to be understood: *Of the motions of a fleet before it is formed into lines or orders; To anchor; To gain the wind; To dispute the wind with the enemy; To avoid an action; To force the enemy into action; To double an enemy; To avoid being doubled; To receive a fleet that bears down upon you,* and so on.

In the same year that O'Bryen published his work a book by vicomte Sébastien Bigot de Morogues, a French naval captain, was translated into English and published as *Naval Tactics, or a Treatise of Evolutions and Signals, with Cuts, lately published in France, for the Use of Cadets, or Guard-Marines of the Academy at Brest, and now established as a complete System of the Marine Discipline of that Nation.* The *Monthly Review* admitted, 'We are so generally supposed to excel our good

---

471 O'Bryen, 1762, v.
472 *Ibid*, vi.
473 *Ibid*, 2.
474 *Ibid*, 16.

neighbours the French in Naval Tactics, that little instruction may perhaps be expected in that art from these our natural enemies... But let us not be so far our own enemies, as to despise instruction because it comes from the French.'[475] The *Review* considered the author of *Naval Tactics* a genius and urged British naval officers to study him, for his work showed the standard of the enemy.

Innovation took time to establish itself but when it did, and if it proved successful, it could alter the means of naval warfare. In 1782 Admiral Rodney fought a French fleet at the Saintes near Dominica. The British fleet cut off the enemy's rearmost ships, captured them and forced the remainder to flee. Eight years later John Clerk's *Essay on Naval Tactics* was published (although he had given unpublished copies to friends as early as 1782[476]) and argued that Rodney's 'breaking the line' had been his idea. Certainly the *Scots Magazine* thought so when it stated in 1805 that 'Rodney broke through at the head of the rear division, and gave the first example of cutting the line. All the consequences predicted by our author immediately ensued... . From this first execution of our author's system, a new æra has been fixed in the history of our naval transactions.'[477]

Clerk gave examples of naval battles from the mid-eighteenth century in which 'neither the difficulty of bringing on an engagement, nor that of pursuing the enemy, arose from any abatement in the spirit of the seamen, nor of any defect in the shipping, on the one side, nor even from any superiority of sailing on the other; but must be attributed alone to the unskilful manner in which the several attacks were conducted.'[478]

He was convinced a new system was wanting, for Royal Navy warships had always sought to find themselves windward of the enemy, to gain the weather-gage, and then go hell for leather. Clerk believed the force of an attack should be concentrated on a 'small portion of the enemy's line'.[479] He thought that for a fleet to approach the enemy in divisions from windward, perhaps towards the rear of the enemy line, might cause the enemy to 'tack in succession' with lead ships at some distance from those so attacked, and if the enemy had to wear then those ships would fall to leeward and so isolate their fellows even further. Clerk also considered attacks made from leeward, and stated, 'nothing promises sucess but the cutting of the enemy's

475 *The Monthly Review Vol XXXVII*, 1767, 464.
476 *The Scots Magazine*, 1805, 852.
477 *Ibid*, 854.
478 Clerk, 1804, xxxvi.
479 Playfair, *ibid,* 450.

line in two.... . The ships thus cut off could have no support, and must either save themselves by downright flight, or fall into the hands of the enemy.'[480]

Within three years of the publication of Clerk's book, Great Britain was again at war. Lord Howe signalled his fleet at the Battle of the Glorious First of June, 1794, to cut the opposite line; Lord St Vincent cut off the enemy division to windward on Valentine's Day 1797 off Cape St Vincent; Lord Duncan cut the Dutch line off Camperdown on 11 October 1797.

In 1801 an article appeared in *The Naval Chronicle* in response to French observations made in a letter to the *Moniteur*. The letter wondered if Clerk, not himself a seaman, had gained his insights from French authors and stated that superior marine force 'when in action, must depend on three things: 1. The better condition of the vessels – 2. The greater naval skill of the officers – 3. The better use of the artillery.'[481] Also, that French ships tended to aim for the rigging, and not the hulls of ships as the British were wont to do. The obvious riposte was for the British author to state how Clerk (written as Clarke) had written a book to the chastisement of Britain's enemies; that Britain had all three 'things' plus the firmness of her seamen who would always stand by their guns whereas the French often did not. 'In short... the hail-storm [of cannon balls]... is the true and only cause of conquest... the irresistible impulse that dismays, disconcerts, and defeats the other party.'[482] The premise was that the enemy might batter British sailors but they themselves would never be subdued.

Clerk added addendums to his book in 1797, which was republished in 1804. A year later the battle of Trafalgar altered things again when 'the combined fleets were drawn up in the form of a crescent, and awaited [the British] attack, which was made in a double column, apparently bearing down upon their centre. This novel mode of coming into action kept the enemy completely in suspense; it threatened every part of their line.'[483]

A belief in the skill and innate stubbornness of the British tar long persisted. 'The superiority of the British in naval tactics, though perhaps never displayed with so dazzling a splendour as at the battle of Trafalgar, has been proved by a long series of triumphs over our enemies. It is natural to ask, whence arises this superiority?'[484] The answer given was not only the skill but the very character of the British. 'From the tempestuous

---

480 *Ibid,* 453.
481 *Naval Chronicle Vol IV*, 1801, 227.
482 *Ibid*, 228.
483 Pantologia, 1813, under Tactics.
484 *Naval Chronicle Vol XIX*, 1808, 225.

nature of our seas, the rapidity of our tides, and the inconstancy of our climate, it may be expected that our mariners, besides being numerous, should be intrepid, dextrous and hardy.'[485] It was a decisive factor because whereas the author argued recent naval achievements were due to 'the system of Rodney, excepting that of Trafalgar' when the line was cut and ships engaged one on one it became more a trial 'of courage, and of nautical and mechanical skill, than of what may be strictly termed naval science'.[486] Nothing, he believed, could hazard natural British nautical grit. So decisive had the British method of cutting the line become that the French Convention government had decreed death to any of their commanders who permitted it to happen.

Also in 1808 Captain John Hampstead published *A Treatise on Naval Tactics*. In the preface he asserted that knowledge of naval tactics was essential to the prosperity of any maritime power, and 'it must therefore naturally excite surprise, that a subject of such great importance should be so little attended to by the generality of officers in the british navy.'[487] This neglect was, he believed, because officers had little or no opportunity to experience a fleet battle or learn the different types of evolution by observation. Instead they had to compass such evolutions in their imagination, a difficult task, 'like trying to solve an intricate question in arithmetic without the aid of pencil or pen'.[488] Mathematical demonstrations, as found in works like Clerk's, were for the author quite tedious. He therefore gave his book three parts: first, plain tactics to be assumed with a steady wind, ships sailing either 'close-hauled on either tack; going free, with the wind on either beam; and going before the wind';[489] second, variable tactics of how wind, fogs and calms affected matters; third, everything surmised by way of an example.

A key aspect of the means by which fleets conducted themselves in battle was the use of signals. A range of flags in combination with pennants, jacks and guns allowed commanders to order quite detailed commands by day; while at night 'signals by lanterns, blue lights, maroons, &c' did the same. Their visual range was extended by use of repeating frigates who signalled an admiral's commands to ships beyond the horizon or those obscured by gunsmoke.

---

485 *Ibid.*
486 *Ibid.*
487 Hampstead, 1808, ix.
488 *Ibid.*
489 *Ibid,* xii.

Before 1799 signals had been drawn up by individual fleet commanders as there was no set system. An anonymous *Essay on Signals* published in 1788 argued that its author had 'many years service, frequent opportunities of remarking the egregious mistakes, and dangerous disappointments, that resulted from the imperfection of Signals [and who had been] induced to try whether improvements might not be made'. A year later Captain West offered his *Naval Signals, constructed on a new Plan,* and in 1790 Lord Howe had devised a numerical system.

In 1799 the Admiralty printed the *Signal-book for the Ships of War* and a companion piece titled *Instructions for the Conducting of Ships of War, explanatory of, and relative to, the Signals contained in the Signal-book herewith delivered.* With colour plates the signal book showed the different flags with their meanings. For instance, a red flag flown alone (signal number 1) meant '*Enemy in sight*'.

Finally, in 1800 Captain Sir Home Popham laid before the government his 'plan for ships corresponding with telegraphs stationed on our coasts'. He had invented a set of flags while onboard the *Romney* (50), and when in India had published a small volume titled *A Marine Vocabulary; or, Telegraphic Signals*, printed in England in 1803.[490]

In early 1815 a retired naval captain, resident of Stoke Damerel, was prompted by the one person who really scared him to write a pamphlet on the nature of naval tactics and signals. Rather than sit tutting at the newspapers, his wife said, *you should write about your experiences.* He flushed with embarrassed meekness, watched his spouse leave the room, then became quite animated with the idea. He might have once roared his will upon ships' compliments, even ordered hundreds of men to action and some to their deaths, but he never could go against her. After a deliberation of seconds – long enough for the woman to depart – he stated to the empty room that whereas he would not write upon naval tactics of the years 1793 to 1815, for he *detested such things!*, he *would present them as a diversion at the Long Room. See if I don't.*

The captain was fully conversant with Clerk. It was, in fact, impossible for him to imagine a time before that essay. When he received the new 1804 edition while at sea he had read the preface in his cabin. When he came across Clerk's admitting of never having been to sea he almost fell off his chair. He certainly cursed loud enough for his steward to pop his head round the door in alarm. After some days of reflection he concluded that

---

490 *The Monthly Magazine*, 1803, 6.

many polymaths imparted knowledge in fields they were never fully part of. Leonardo da Vinci knew much about the human body by cutting them up but had never, so far as he knew, practiced medicine. So Clerk remained an authority for him.

Together with other books, his own experience and a readiness for the subject the captain felt capable of success. A piece in *Cobbett's Political Register* of 1812 spurred him on: 'A battle at sea is an affair of ropes and sails and rudders. The victory depends, in a great measure, upon the dexterity of the parties engaged.'[491] *Yes,* he had harrumphed at the time, *the more alert, prepared and drilled a ship's crew the better it is. And there is more to it than that. There are maneuvers and tactics. But those adequate for a ship of the line might not be suitable for a frigate. Do people not realise this?*

The more he thought about it the more the project appealed. He imagined a gala night for naval officers and the general public, one useful for civilians to learn facts. For example: the worst thing any ship or vessel could do at sea was to present itself prow or stern on to an enemy broadside. Fifteen, twenty, or God forbid fifty guns firing down the expanse of a ship's deck was a nightmare no sailor ever wished to experience. Furthermore, 'the masts and shrouds, from being seen in a line, and the whole space, from the situation, being quadruply darkened with rigging, a shot taking place in that area, therefore, must carry away something of considerable consequence; and a shot... must rake the men from one end of the ship to another.'[492] The horror of being raked. He had done it to an enemy more than once and had been raked by two ships in battle himself.

What of a fleet? How dangerous it was for one to sail before the wind, laid out in line ahead, to avoid an enemy in pursuit! Woe betide any ship in the rear for they would be far removed from the assistance of the ships in the van who would have to turn and tack upon tack against the wind to reach them.

So he began to plan for his great presentation. An introduction, numerous segments and a conclusion were all laid out. He said to himself, *certainly the weather-gage must be mentioned.* For large engagements he thought he would show the way line of battle ships formed parallel lines to one another, on the same tack or not, until one ship fought its opposite. But how could he convey that effectively to an audience? *How do I show a whole fleet in*

---

491 *Cobbett's Political Register*, 1812, 257.
492 Clerk, *ibid*, 24.

a line of battle – so formed to allow every ship to be part of the action and not be blocked by another – make its approach to an enemy, made supine as they lay-to, with our line and guns almost at ninety degrees to the wind? What of exposure, problems of rear ships joining battle, certain decided disadvantages? Hmmm.

One afternoon an idea came to him like a thunderbolt thrown by Zeus. *Yes, that will suffice!* Somehow he persuaded his wife to sit for one short session while he explained to her possible approaches a ship might make against another. She sat stone silent throughout while he set up small blocks of wood on the dinner table – *worry not, my dear, this canvas will protect the surface, do you see?* – and explained how each block represented a ship with one end narrowed for the prow.

'Now, my dear,' he said, 'let us consider two lone ships, one ours and t'other the enemy's. They meet and are of equal strength. Great care must be taken to not allow the enemy to rake our ship. See how I move them on parallel courses? Our stout British ship here approaches the vile enemy – so badly handled with scrubs of officers and rancid smelling men – at small angles in an attempt to keep her broadside towards the other. Our ship should not approach the enemy too quickly by means of turning her prow towards her broadside, like so, for she would expose herself to unnecessary hurt. If the enemy were to fire she could dismast our ship or cut swathes of ropes. Instead our ship should approach astern of the enemy in its wake, getting there by narrow angles. A slow affair, but by so doing only a few enemy stern-chasers could be fired in their defence. Deftly handled our British ship is able to turn at will. See how I do so, at ninety degrees? Only for a quick time to expel a full broadside before I turn her back to the wake and so continue with the chase. She can repeat this as often as she likes if she is a good sailer and the wind remains true. But of course if our ship turns to offer her broadside and the enemy ship ahead wears to offer her broadside it would be towards our ship's rear so it is a risk...'

When he looked up, for the first time since he began his demonstration, he saw his wife sporting a deep frown, so he thanked her for her time and she was soon gone. He dared not ask her again.

For the next practice, *Should We Aim for Rigging or the Hull of a Ship?* the house cat was cajoled into sitting on a chair with the lure of a cushion and some fish. But complaints followed about how it made the room stink. *The Merits of Disabling Enemy Rigging with Respect to How the Enemy Becomes Incapacitated* was stated to his grandson's toy soldiers. *What Should a Line of Battleships do if another Line of Battleships lays to*

Windward? was given to a corn dolly propped up on a chair, but he forgot to remove her and she was broken when his wife sat on her at dinner. Finally, he hit on a compromise. With his *Lying to, to Receive an approaching Enemy Line* he placed a line of brown bottles with wooden circles taped to their necks upon the chairs, the circles daubed with badly drawn but appreciative faces. No complaints afterwards, for the bottles had been cleaned and were big enough for him to remember to stow them away. They thereafter became his audience, his 'bottlemen'.

He had to admit that he had missed every large naval battle of the era, being a captain of frigates on distant stations, and so lacked superior knowledge. His saving grace was his books and contacts; he was on good terms with the port admiral, Sir William Domett, and he often ventured round to meet him with either a pot of his wife's sherry marmalade or a selection of comfits. These did the trick and he managed to get snippets about the admiral's experiences at the Saintes, the Siege of Gibraltar and the Glorious First of June. He regretted mentioning Copenhagen. 'Copenhagen!' barked the admiral, who stood up out of his chair and limped around the room.[493] 'I was abused, sir, abused! Pray do not talk of this again.' When the captain returned home, worried and despondent, it suddenly struck him that the admiral had not been mentioned in dispatches at the time. Thankfully, his blunder caused no lasting damage, for his wife's marmalade was so very good.

At first he was too technical, for he wished to be on par with Clerk. *We see the van of B, having attained their station at A, that is, a-breast of the van of F... in their fire upon the van of B... as instructed by F, shall bear away in succession, as at H.*[494] For him evolutions on paper were easy to follow and his bottlemen never complained. Yet when moving his blocks about before a live audience, in this case neighbours who came round for tea, they soon lost track. When he lit a mass of cloth to make smoke, his wife glared at him and brought the session to an immediate end. Although his guests smiled and thanked him, he knew it had been a disaster.

Quickly he learned not to mention steerage, command of the rudder, distance apart, the wind shifting, partial breezes, contrariness and the sea-state. Civilian audiences obviously cared little for such things. Nor the 'difficulty of bringing opponent fleets to close engagement'.[495] Instead he

---

493 He complained of a lame foot and retired because of it.
494 Clerk, *ibid*, 33.
495 *Ibid*, 36.

adopted simple language and simple ideas. It was enough that every ship sailed perfectly in perfect formation on perfect seas. *Do you see we have two sets of ships? These black blocks are the enemy. These white ones are our wonderful wooden wall. Note the small notches on their sides, they are the guns.* When he hit upon a slanted stand to raise up his blocks he felt his audience would be better able to follow his ideas. And when showing repeating frigates about the line of battleships he amused himself that he would state them to be similar to Sancho Panza attendant upon Don Quixote.

Wind formed the basis of almost all naval considerations. He intended to talk about it. Even to repeat himself. *What of the advantages and disadvantages of the fabled weather gage?* For a ship to be windward of an enemy meant it could approach at will and decide whether to 'accelerate or delay the beginning of the engagement'.[496] In company with a larger force, fire-ships or smoke could be sent over to annoy the enemy rear and make a distraction. Boarding was made an easier proposition. But there was the risk that if a ship had to retreat it would be required to pass close by the enemy, even through an enemy line, and the foe thereby gained advantage of the wind. If dismasted the risk was all the greater, which had once happened to his old ship.

Where he felt real confidence was with his conclusion, which he rehearsed many times. He thought only the navy a true means of national security. He decided to state how *we stand alone as an island girthed by the sea, so in the first instance a conflict must always be conducted by the navy! We can only ever rely on our warships to defend our shores. What had Joseph Gander written so long ago?* 'And 'tis a universal Maxim... . Whosoever Commands the Sea, Commands the Trade of the World; He that Commands the Trade of the World, Commands the Wealth of the World, and consequently the World itself... . so he that is Master of the Sea, may... be said to be Master of every Country; at least such as are bordering on the Sea; For he is at liberty to begin and end War, where, when, and on what Terms he pleaseth, and extend his Conquests even to the Antipodes.'[497]

Being a man of the times, he intended to extol the virtues of British seamen: their discipline, ability to break the line and superior gunnery. *As our ships plough the sea British tars are unquenchable! They are the Prime Mover of the nation. They maintain our interest and control the seas. Their very presence is enough to break the ardour of an enemy,*

---

496 Campbell, 1813, 416/17.
497 Gander, 1703, 1.

even if in superior numbers! For they know of our courage, discipline and perseverance.[498] *Our practice of cutting the line is so very simple, yet based on such sound common sense. There are no scoundrel tricks involved. We will always beat the enemy so long as we can get at them to fight a fair fight! Above all, proved tactics, as I have demonstrated here tonight, make the wooden wall both our senior service and our saviour! With good commanders, good pay and victuals the navy will defy the devil!*[499]

He planned to finish with questions and so prepared himself. If any cynic dared bring up the issue of the American war he would silently damn their eyes, smile, and state how that yes, the Americans had captured in order the *Alert* (18), *Guerrière* (38), *Frolic* (18), *Macedonian* (38), *Java* (38), *Peacock* (18), *Boxer* (14), *Epervier* (18), *Reindeer* (18), *Avon* (18), *Cyane* (22), *Levant* (20) and *Penguin*; but the British had taken the *Wasp* (18), *Chesapeake* (38), *Argus* (20), *Essex* (32), *Frolic* (22) and *President* (50)[500] as well as recaptured the *Avon* and *Levant*! The Royal Navy remained above all others!

As the evening approached he convinced himself it would be a wonderful night. Most of his invited guests were to be present and Plymouth residents were ever eager to learn about the navy. When his wife stated in cold terms she would not be able to attend he blustered how sad he was, bowed meekly and when alone smiled so wide his cheeks hurt. Yes, it would be a splendid evening.

---

498 Similar to words found in *The Scots Magazine*, 1805, 855.
499 Similar to words found in *Remarks on the Present Condition of the Navy*, 1700, 13.
500 Brighton, 1866, xi.

Chapter 9

Still more Majestic Shalt thou Rise

The boatman had never seen so many happy people. Neither had he known so much business. Either at the Torpoint ferry, the steps at Dock, Mutton Cove, Mill Bay or Sutton Pool. There were hundreds of people eager to purchase any boat to take them out to the sound. Despite all competition as he pulled up he had no trouble gaining customers, for his wherry was the most highly festooned of all with bunting, ribbons and flags a-plenty. He himself might have deterred people with one eye lost and a disfigured jaw but he looked the part for such a unique time – he sported a top hat with a British flag tied around it and a French flag wrapped around his stomach like a Persian cummerbund. He was obviously a naval invalid and his mannerisms, strong smell of tobacco and rum and dark weathered features stated clearly to everyone he had fought for king and country. His three boys were dressed in a similar manner and as soon as any woman saw their bright faces and downy locks she could not hire the boat quick enough.

He had other means of income. At night he allowed drunks to hit him on the good side of his face for a small fee. He was an ex-pugilist and no one had done him serious hurt. But it was a meagre living and suddenly with the great man coming to town rich pickings were to be made.

At dawn on Sunday he pushed his boat out into the river and let the tide take it down towards Mount Edgcumbe and the Cremyll Ferry. He steered for Mutton Cove and landed in front of a large excited crowd and easily gained six passengers. The four women were like geese while the two men tried to show quiet importance but failed when getting into the boat. They paid their fees, gave him a tip to row dry[501], and the boat was pushed out with the help of men who loitered near the inn.

Through the Crimble Passage they joined a procession of boats and one of his passengers remarked how quick the tide took them. They did indeed race past Devil's Point. He made sure they gave German Rock a wide berth and they

---

501 without splashing water into the boat.

had the usual hard pull between Drake's Island and the Hoe before edging out into the Sound. All around them were hundreds of boats and small vessels intent on the same destination. The noise was loud and raucous but good natured, and some people were already drinking from bottles. A loud voice came across the water: *At least we'll see him this time, Mary, not like at Torbay.*

Ahead lay the *Billy Ruffian*, tall amongst a mass of boats that had already taken the good spots. He did not worry about that for he carried weight amongst boatmen and they would let him through soon enough. A little delay at some distance increased his customers' excitement, enough so that when they returned they would give a decent pay-off. And if they ever looked like they would not, then a tale of his adventures on a warship and the loss of his wife – *the poor boys' mother, God bless her soul* – would encourage them to spill a few extra pennies.

As they approached the *Bellerophon* his passengers were beside themselves. One woman pointed a fat hand and shouted, 'There he is! There! See him in his great grey coat?'

'I see him! Ah, so that's him. A tyrant if ever there was one. Everything to him was a campaign.'

'Everything?'

'Yes, dear. Everything.'

The women giggled for these last words were said in a knowing and suggestive manner. When the famous Frenchman raised his hat at a beautiful young woman in the boat ahead all the women thereabouts cooed with delight; apart from one old matriarch who complained, *No foreigner will impugn my dignity.*

Napoléon stood high above them on the deck of the 74, his stature small and squat, and he was definitely on show. The crowd gave him the respect they would an exhibit in a ceremonial levée.[502] But the boatman started to worry. There were more people than he thought possible. Some female passengers stood and waved their handkerchiefs. Others rocked their boats dangerously. Oars clashed and waters splashed. He instinctively looked towards the *Billy Ruffian* and an officer trumpeted orders to the assembled guard-boats below. They became aggressive for they had a prisoner to protect, and who could say whether this was all a ruse? They rammed nearby pleasure boats that dared venture too close and threatened to tip passengers into the water. This was no festive season for them.

---

502 *The Western Antiquary,* 1882, 199. It refers to the words of Sir Charles Eastlake who painted a picture of Bonaparte on the *Bellerophon.*

The nearest boats had to back their oars which forced others to do the same. It turned ugly. They collided twice, and one of the men in the boat trapped a hand as a boat flew by. Over all the commotion he heard an accented voice from the *Bellerophon* complain, *Is this English liberty?* But they had won, hadn't they? Let the people enjoy the moment! They were civilians amongst a flotilla of warships so what could they do? The two frigates nearby might turn their guns on them if it continued.

The crowd settled, all the boats rocked, and once more hundreds of eyes gazed with curiosity on the presence of Old Boney. There was no animosity or disgust. The French general had been a man of the moment, a force of nature, one who dominated the age.

All too soon the object of their interest disappeared below deck. Apart from the one who nursed a red raw hand, the boatman's passengers were very satisfied for this was a day they would long remember. He gave the nod to his boys and they began the long pull home. The tide had slackened but they were exhausted by the time they dropped off their customers at Mutton Cove. His customers did give extra, for he had told them how his *wife had been taken a prisoner by French privateers some years back, never to be seen again, but praise be to God for his boys who acted as his lost eye, so to speak.* The one who hurt his hand gave him an odd look, more for doubting the story than anything else.

After his passengers walked off he gave a few pennies to the men ashore and they pushed the boat back into midstream. The boatman and his sons' day was nearly over so he reached below the sheets and took out a bottle of brandy. He bit the cork and pulled it out, took a full swig with the cork still in his mouth, handed the bottle to his sons, and on its return replaced the cork and hid the bottle away again.

'So, lads. Let's go home by way of the butcher, eh?' He fancied a nice cut of lamb for dinner and his wife was such a good cook.

His boys cheered and amongst a flotilla of other boats they continued to the Hamoaze. As they rowed he had time to consider what exactly the capture of Old Boney meant for the likes of him and his family. The long war was finally over. Twenty years of his life had been spent at sea and at war. He had the scars to prove it: a jaw broken off Brest, thanks to a yard that fell from above; a toe lost during a cutting out expedition on the Spanish coast at some place he had never heard of; a ball taken in the leg at Tenerife; an eye lost to a snapped rope off Ireland. As they beached to walk to the nearest butcher the boatman smiled to himself. It had been a profitable day. Tomorrow they would do it all over again, for there would be more passengers eager to see Bonaparte.

He and his boys tried to ignore the mass of homeless innocents huddled beside a low wall.

Napoléon claimed that he had boarded the *Bellerophon* (74)[503] a free man and not a prisoner. He thought himself 'the guest of England'.[504] In a letter dated 4 August 1815 he stated, 'I appeal to history; - it will say that an enemy, who made war for twenty years upon the English people, came voluntarily in his misfortunes to seek asylum under their laws... But what return did England make for so magnanimous an act?'[505] By then he knew he was for exile in the South Atlantic.

The *Bellerophon* had been part of the Rochefort blockade squadron that departed for home with her unexpected guest as soon as Bonaparte and his suite had settled. By all accounts they proved affable and lively and quite fascinated the crew. The highland of Dartmoor was seen on 23 July 1815 and next morning the ship was off Dartmouth. When Bonaparte first saw Torbay he considered it to be similar to Portoferraio on Elba. Lord Keith was aboard the *Ville de Paris* (110) and he put an immediate embargo on the *Bellerophon*. No one was allowed on or off except for himself and Sir John Duckworth. But nothing could remain hidden for long and the *Bellerophon* was soon crowded with boats full of locals eager to get a glimpse of the extraordinary Frenchman. He was seldom hidden from view as he liked to stand on deck or peer out a window to allow the appreciative crowds to gratify their curiosity. He often raised his hat at the ladies. Baskets of fruit and letters begging for an audience arrived onboard but all were refused. On 26 July the ship was ordered to proceed to Plymouth Sound.

On arrival in Plymouth Bonaparte was impressed with the breakwater. He considered it a 'great national undertaking, and highly honourable to the country'.[506] Despite orders from the admiralty to deter boats from approaching more than a cable length of the *Bellerophon*, and placing frigates either side of her in case of an attempt to make a rescue, hundreds of people approached the sides of the captive's ship. The Frenchman remarked how well dressed the ladies were. It was a festive gala and anyone able to purchase a boat dressed in their finest, for it was not every day they came across an Emperor.

---

503 15 July 1815.
504 Bourienne, 1885, 385.
505 *Ibid.*
506 *The Western Antiquary,* ibid, 198.

The largest press of people appeared Sunday, 30 July 1815, when some 1,000 people turned up, loud and raucous with boats each carrying at least six people. Guard boats struggled to fend them off, and this kind of tumult continued for days.

On 3 August 1815 something odd was in the air for Bonaparte failed to appear at breakfast. The *Eurotas* (38) was consulted for any possible sign, none seen, so a midshipman was made to peer through a window and see if the great man sat in his chair. When an orderly went into his cabin on some pretext, Bonaparte was found to be ill in bed. After that scare the *Bellerophon* was made ready to sail upon an instant.

The *Billy Ruffian* ought to have sailed to St Helena with Bonaparte and his permitted suite but she was too old and in need of repair. Therefore she sailed out of Plymouth with the *Tonnant* (80) on 7 August 1815 to meet the *Northumberland* (74) and two troopships off Berry Head. Lord Keith was in the barge and Admiral Cockburn waited aboard his new ship to accompany Napoléon to his final exile. He was transferred with full honours. It signalled the end of hostilities and of the era. 'The glorious termination of the war excited a degree of enthusiastic joy in the British dominions of which it is impossible to give an adequate idea.'[507] Rapturous were those who had lived to see the end; for many it had been their whole lives.

Peace had been made with the United States and the manning of the Royal Navy for 1815 was reduced by more than half from 144,000 to 70,000 men. The immediate benefits of lower costs were not felt because when all the released men arrived home, together with regiments from abroad, they had to be paid off at an expense to the nation higher than any other year of the war.[508] Charges for the navy in 1815 stood at '14,897,000*l*' with a further '3,747,000*l*' for transports.[509]

Thirty years later a Plymouth judge of long standing took his leave due to persistent rheumatism. His doctor ordered him to take the waters at Bath; and whereas his gavel colleagues tried to dissuade him from going, saying he could do just as well drinking salt water at home and who in their right mind would put up with the travel, decided to go for he was utterly fed up with the local weather. As he packed his portmanteau he began a long, disjointed conversation with himself upon the ways Plymouth, the Royal Navy and the United Kingdom had all altered since his childhood. He considered himself old school and loved the navy, but it was only after

---

507 Alison, 1855, 488.
508 *The Annual Register*, 1815, 45.
509 *Ibid*, 36.

many years that one could fully comprehend what the senior service had been between the years 1801 and 1815.

To begin with, the navy had been sustained by the nation and had in turn sustained her. The price paid was steep. *Ahh, the fall of Bonaparte. I stood there on shore with spyglass in hand and saw him on deck. The flame of outright war might have been extinguished but other laments could be heard. Instead of death rattles of the fallen, howls of the injured and exhausted complaints of those on blockade, there were the sighs of the workless, rumbles of hunger and moans of poverty. Men and women of little or no means cheered for victory but were fearful of the future. How could so many without employment be expected to survive? Inopiae desunt multa.*[510]

Numerous business failures followed war's end, corn prices fell and a 'general depression' ensued.[511] Exhausted by so many years of war, enterprise and industry needed to rouse themselves back to action. The *Annual Register*'s preface for 1815 stated, 'it is to be apprehended that a remote period must be assigned as that of the recovery of the national prosperity.'[512] *A remote period indeed. Even now I am not convinced it has been achieved. Those who fell to harsh necessity increased week by week and many of them appeared in court. There was never enough alms to dole out and people had to survive somehow. More than a few had fought and worked fiercely for their country, but were forgotten in peace. Ubi servitutem faciunt, pacem appellant.*[513] *Has it not always been so?*

How the national condition altered. Back in 1793, when war with revolutionary France first erupted, his father's farm and business prospered. The enemy's sea commerce was decimated to the betterment of their own, thanks to the Royal Navy, and it had been drilled into him: *destroy the enemy, take their colonies, increase our trade!* There followed years of wealth and increased manufactures. People flocked to Plymouth to seek employment. The local population increased, as did the need to provide corn to feed them. His father opened up new fields and hired more men and most of the farm's produce ended up at the victualling office in Plymouth. Rents increased and prices rose. Away at university it was much the same, except his studies there caused the outside world to recede into a fog that only re-formed on his return home. The 1813 crop had been abundant[514] but most

---

510 *To poverty many things are lacking.*

511 *The Annual Register, ibid.*

512 *Ibid*, 1815, vi.

513 *They create desolation and call it peace.*

514 *The Edinburgh Annual Register,* 1817, 60.

previous ones had not, so people went hungry; and national expenditure on the Peninsula campaign was more than had ever been spent before.

Peace returned and, like a deflated balloon, agriculture and national prosperity declined. The army and navy no longer required so much produce or materials. Many faced a precarious future. Sailors of the northern coal trade rioted over their wages and followed a course similar to 'that in the [1797] naval mutiny'.[515] Authorities intervened when they closed the Tyne river to traffic. Thankfully, little violence ensued. That same year there were further riots due to the new Corn Bill. Farmers of the South Hams and on Dartmoor became insolvent. How his mother had cried when his father sold off half the farm.

In 1816 it was decided a vast navy was no longer required. A 'great number of ships and vessels were sold or broken up. This reduction in the numerical amount of the navy consisted of one ship of eighty guns, ten of seventy-four, and eight of sixty-four; three of 50-gun ships; six frigates of thirty-eight, eight of thirty-six, six of thirty-two, and three of twenty-eight guns... [etc] making altogether nineteen ships of the line, and ninety-three ships and vessels of inferior rates.'[516]

The British people had to deal 'with the prospect of want and pauperism before their eyes as what must be their destiny at last... [that] in the road that the English labourer must travel, the poor house is the last stage on the way to the grave.'[517] *It was as though the nation assumed an opposite visage to the then king: the mind of authority and business slowly improved but the body politic was alienated and not always tranquil. It was certainly not salus populi suprema lex esto.*[518]

There had been riots in Glasgow and Sheffield, and the poor of Brighton had to be supplied with bread and meat by the Prince Regent himself.[519] Around the country debtors' prisons admitted new inmates. *A Report from the Select Committee on the Poor Laws: with the Minutes of Evidence taken before the Committee; and an Appendix* was published 4 July 1817; and a *Report of the Lords' Committees, on the Poor Laws; with Minutes of Evidence* was published 10 July 1817. The judge read them more than once and agreed that 'The general distress of the last two years, which

---

515 *The Annual Register*, ibid, 141.

516 Fincham, 1851, 191.

517 Walsh, 1819, 410.

518 *The welfare of the people is the highest law.*

519 *The European Magazine*, 1817, 68/9. The riot in Glasgow took place on 1 August 1816, that in Sheffield 3 December 1816.

perhaps never was equalled in a country civilized like ours... has naturally turned all eyes upon the causes, moral or political, which appear to have contributed towards it.'[520] It was thought by some that the Poor Laws added to the distress. He apprehended that whereas many ex-naval seamen gained employment with the merchant trade most could not, for the commercial fleet likewise shrunk. *Deus vult.*[521]

He knew all about the plight of the poor as he had been involved with their relief. Ever since the time of Queen Anne there had been *An Act for the erecting a Workhouse in the Town and Borough of Plymouth, in the County of Devon, and for setting the Poor to work, and maintaining them there.*[522] As he sat on the edge of his bed, quite fagged out with packing his things, he thought of the report published only a few weeks before that argued workhouses were needed for 'the removal of the great mischiefs arising from such number of unemployed poor'.[523] *True. Without employment a man is in need and the means to fulfil such need often causes him to break the law. Given the beneficence of the borough it is upsetting to think so many remain ungrateful.* Many of the Poor's Portion in Plymouth were ex-seamen who often complained to him of their lot. One old sea-dog moaned, 'For breakfast yesterday I had but one quart of milk broth with oats, and a dinner of boiled beef and potatoes with a scrap of cabbage and a supper of thin broth which dinner had been a-boiled in. I drown in thin broth, sir! And look to these mad-men here, they act worse than any foreign prisoner you would find.'

A number of warships were ordered to be built, for the Royal Navy had to remain prepared for any future conflict. On 28 July 1816, ten warships, five brigs, and four bomb vessels sailed out of Plymouth Sound for Algiers to deal with corsairs[524] and John Croker, First Secretary to the Admiralty,[525] created a Reserve Fleet. But with the overall reduction of the fleet many once formidable warships were cast down. The *Bellerophon* was made a prison hulk in 1819 off Sheerness. That had saddened him. *What have we come to? The* Billy Ruffian *took Bonaparte prisoner!* But few people then cared for such matters and many of *Bellerophon's* battle sisters ended their

520 *The British Review, and the London Critical Journal*, 1817, 350.
521 *God wills it.*
522 *Annual Report of the Poor Law Commissioners for England and Wales*, 1844, 83.
523 *Annual Report of the Poor Law Commissioners for England and Wales, ibid.* The sea-dogs diet comes from this same source, page 104.
524 *Brett's Illustrated Naval History of Great Britain*, 1871, 315.
525 He fulfilled the position once taken by Evan Nepean who left office in 1804.

careers as sad carcasses stripped of ordnance, masts and dignity, cast into some dismal creek or inlet.

This horrid means to house prisoners began at the time of the first American War when the *Justitia*, an 'old Indiaman, and the "Censor," a frigate, were the first floating prisons established in England'.[526] In January 1841 it was found that 3,552 convicts were interned on various hulks. By the time the judge decided to go to Bath this had fallen to 1,298.[527] Three were under the age of 10, and 213 under the age of 15. The *Warrior* hulk, an old 74-gun warship, suffered 38 deaths in 1841.

The judge's thoughts returned to 1816 when it became obvious the Navy had moved away from certain regulations and practices. The admiralty admitted the rating of warships had never been officially formalised. So *Proposals and Regulations relative to the Royal Navy* made by the Board of Admiralty and sanctioned by Order in Council on 1st January 1817 were introduced because 'it was impossible, during the pressure of war, either to resist the innovations which temporary circumstances rendered necessary, or to re-mould and reform the whole system of the navy, on every occasion on which some alteration was introduced.'[528] The rates of naval ships, fixed since the time of Charles I, were reclassified to state the number of guns and carronades carried. *Lord knows why nobody thought of that before. Seldom have I read two reports that agree to the number of guns carried in a battle.* He had read William James on 'the revival... of the ancient and only reasonable practice of rating the ships'.[529] *Because that was the thing, it* was *the only reasonable practice.* A first rate was set to have 100 or more guns; a second rate 80 plus guns on two decks; a third rate 70 to 80 guns; a fourth rate 50 to 70 guns; a fifth rate 36 to 50 guns and a sixth rate 24 to 36 guns. No ship under 24 guns was to be classified as a post-ship,[530] that is a ship commanded by a captain proper.

As to the manning of ship's complements, the Order in Council stated it was a bag of happenstance, thanks to foreign captures often being larger than British ships of a similar class, and was especially impracticable with sixth rates. Third rates alone had 'seven distinct complements'. Twenty-nine schemes for manning were therefore reduced to fourteen.[531]

---

526 Mayhew, 1862, 199.

527 *Ibid.*

528 *The Edinburgh Annual Register for 1817*, 1821, 234.

529 James, 1824, 589.

530 *The Edinburgh Annual Register for 1817*, 237.

531 Manning for sloops remained an issue then not finalised.

For those who had served, their pay and organisation was much improved and made easier to account for. All commissioned, warrant and petty officers were paid dependent on the rate of ship they served on, so a captain of a first rate received £800 nett per annum whereas a captain of a sixth rate received £350.[532] The allowance of a commander's table money was increased. Some ratings were introduced and some abolished. Companies of Royal Marine artillery, formed in 1804 to man bomb-vessels, were increased to eight companies.

An issue of 'serious injury to the service' was how 'irregularities and deviation from establishment in regard to the form, scantling, &c. of his Majesty's ships'[533] had brought about excessive costs to supply masts and yards, rope and stores of various dimensions and construction. There was little standardisation and a mast or yard for one ship was often useless for another unless great labour, time and effort was given to alter them. This resulted in a sluggish provision of refit, an overstocked set of naval arsenals and a squadron of ships that had to be individually supplied at great cost. Until 1817 this was considered *nervos belli, pecuniam infinitam.*[534] When he remembered how the admiralty had addressed the Prince Regent on this problem it had struck him how dutifully obedient they were: 'We beg leave humbly to assure your Royal Highness, that no efforts shall be spared on our parts, to prevent for the future, any unnecessary deviation from the establishment of rigging and armament, and to reduce the variations which exist to as few classes as possible.'[535]

The years had flowed by but the old evil of impressment remained, despite Parliament debating *de novo* this sad aspect of the naval world. In the great war against France it had been deemed a necessary burden but with peace some wondered whether it should continue.[536] He personally detested the brutal means of recruitment. *Tu ne cede malis, sed contra audentior ito.*[537] *What of voluntary service? If the navy offered better rates of pay and bounties, with shorter periods of service, then there would be no need for impressment.* The Seaman's Registration Act of 30 July 1835 brought about some improvements as it ensured that no pressed man could serve more than five years and criminals were barred from serving on warships, as 'the

532 *The Edinburgh Annual Register for 1817*, 241.

533 *The Edinburgh Annual Register for 1817*, 238.

534 *Endless money is the sinew of war.*

535 *The Annual Register,* 1818, 343.

536 Erskine May, 1878, 24.

537 *Yield not to misfortunes, but go boldly against them.*

service should not be disgraced by having vagabonds mixed with honest men.'[538] But as John Gourly contended, it did not get rid of the 'swell mob... crimps and screws, who rob the seamen and their employers... for these scamps are the great cause of all the disorder, drunkenness, and desertion amongst our seamen.'[539] The judge had summed it up at the time as, *It only goes to show how awful things used to be.*

A major change, albeit a slow one, was with the construction of warships. In the latter years of the great war foreign supplies of wood, specifically Canadian oak, had been found to decay earlier than timber imported from the Baltic. In 1812 'the *Devonshire* was planked with [this] timber, which, in 1817, was totally decayed.'[540] For John Fincham and others, suitable alternatives were Italian oak, teak, and British larch. Whatever the wood, warships were strengthened due to Robert Seppings' system of diagonal timbering.[541] Trialled before the end of the war, in 1815 HMS *Howe* (120-gun) was the first to be constructed to his ideas. The judge had known officers who served on her and they told him how very sound she was.[542] Warships thereafter were ordered to be built with circular prow and stern, the stern being especially important for 'the danger of being pooped [was] considerably diminished'.[543]

Distrusted by naval officers steeped in an age of sail, steamships were kept at bay for years. Old ways and skills remained so that the Navy of 1824 was little changed from that of 1793. However in 1825 the 'Government... attached to each of the dock-yards one or more steam-vessels, of the most substantial build, and of great power, for towing ships out and into harbour.... where a ship, squadron, or fleet, may often be required to put hastily to sea.'[544] Two years later, Navarino[545] proved to be the last battle fought entirely by sailing ships. Of the combined British, French and Russian fleet the British had the *Asia* (84); the 74s *Albion* and *Genoa*; the 40s *Cambrian and Glasgow; Dartmouth (36); Talbot* (28); *Hind* (20); *Rose* (18); the 10s *Brisk, Musquito* and *Philomel.*

Captain John Ross of the navy wrote, in 1828, a *Treatise on Navigation by Steam.* He argued steam was 'more applicable to naval warfare than to

---

538 Gourly, 47.

539 Gourly, 1838, iii.

540 Fincham, 1851, 217.

541 James, 1886, 298.

542 James wrote, 'there is not... a sounder ship in the British navy', p. 299.

543 James.

544 *Blackwood's Edinburgh Magazine,* 1825, 543.

545 1827.

commercial purposes'[546] and discussed possible tactics for steam warships. They could be made to weather heavy seas 'without damage either to the wheels or the machinery', be fortified from shot, and because of their lower cost of production and better efficiency would force the government to 'suffer steam ships to supercede the whole British navy'. [547]

The judge, finishing his packing, had read that steam-powered warships made 'Great Britain more powerful than ever she was at any former period of her history'[548] and wondered whether the wooden wall would one day turn into an iron wall. *Firebrand* (6), a wooden-hulled paddle-driven frigate, was now in her seventh year of service, and the *Cyclops* (6) her fifth. Other wooden-hulled paddle ships were soon to join them: the *Terrible* (20); the 10s *Avenger* and *Retribution*; the 6s *Dragon*, *Centaur*, *Gladiator* and *Vulture*; the *Sampson* (4) and the *Penelope* refitted to be a 22-gun paddle-ship frigate. The *Terrible* and *Avenger* were then being built in Devonport and when he first saw them he did not know what to make of their half-dome paddle boxes and black funnels. The wooden-hulled screw-driven frigates, *Rattler* (9), the 5s *Polyphemus* and *Prometheus*, and the *Alecto* (4) were also under construction. On reflection he did not doubt that soon enough wooden hulls would disappear. *In the end it will not be the enemy that destroyed the wooden wall but iron.*

His bedroom had a dozen or so shelves heaped with dog-eared naval history books. A whole raft of them had been published in the past thirty years, together with memoirs and reports, devoted to the war years 1793 to 1815. He had read most of them and some passages remained fixed in his memory brighter than any poem or song. The more florid the language the better: 'The royal navy of England hath ever been its greatest defence and ornament; it is its ancient and natural strength; the floating bulwark of the island; and army, from which, however strong and powerful, no danger can ever be apprehended to liberty; and accordingly it has been assiduously cultivated, even from the earliest ages.'[549]

One shelf stood out for him: a thick oaken beam taken off a fifth rate that carried slim volumes of naval abstracts. He knew them intimately and could see in his mind's eye their contents. Numbers and scraps of words which showed, running from left to right, the increase then decrease then increase

---

546 *The Southern Review,* 1830, 198.
547 *Ibid.*
548 Gourly, 1838, iv.
549 Vincent Wanostrocht, 1823, 134.

again of the fleet and its expense. *Abstract of the Navy estimates for the Year 1825*[550] *- Wages, victuals, wear and tear, and ordnance, for 29,000 men... £1,941,555.0.0. Ordinary estimate... £3,415,588.17.10. Extra estimate... £625,988.0. Near on six millions of pounds sterling. Abstracts for the Year 1840... . There shall be applied 5,824,974l. For naval services... for 35,165 seamen and marines.*[551] It was ever a case of *tempora mutantur, nos et mutamur in illis.*[552] The books also showed that the manning for the navy was well below that of the army. For instance, in 1827 it was voted 30,000 men for the Sea Service and 9,000 Royal Marines, while the army was voted 87,000 men. New, better-built ships needed smaller complements and the empire required garrisons.

In 1824 the yard and town of Dock had changed so much that it was renamed Devonport. He was present on 12 August at the laying of the foundation stone for a new plinth to commemorate this event. Even now, years later, he struggled to call the place Devonport. He disliked how it shut a door on the past. *It had been Dock that helped keep the French in their own ports far away from English shores. What could be more appropriate a name for a naval yard? Dock! It proclaimed that this was a place of the navy. It was a name for a warlike enterprise. Devonport? Ahh, such is change –* vanitas vanitatum omnia vanitas.[553]

But he had to admit that some changes were for the better. As he carried his things downstairs he thought to himself, *After 1815 the navy became a different proposition: smaller, sleeker, and better organised. When I think of how things were back then to how they are now, so many improvements have been made. Navigation and hydrography, victuals, pay, terms of service, stronger and faster ships. The navy is ever a burden, but also a boon and a blessing and no other nation compares. Britain truly did and does rule the waves. Rule Britannia!*

As the old judge left Plymouth, never to return, he felt both excited and sad. All this introspection and the aches in his bones made him perceive the relentless passage of time. For Great Britain cum United Kingdom of Great Britain and Ireland her armed forces had always been there to protect her; most of all the Royal Marines and the Royal Navy.

The wooden wall had started to fade. Wind was being abandoned for steam. He began to hear more and more the term senior service used in

---

550 *Parliamentary abstracts*, 1826, 513.

551 *A Compendious Abstract of the Public General Acts,* 1840, 277.

552 *Times change and we change with them.*

553 Vanity, vanity, everything vanity.

conversation[554] but was aware of complaints made by naval medical officers that their rank was beneath that of their brethren in the army. At times neglected and abused, the Royal Navy remained ever faithful and ready for service whenever the call should come. He was certain it would remain so in the future. *Si vis pacem, para bellum.*[555]

---

554 The term 'senior service' was certainly in use by 1849, as in *The Medical Times Vol 19*, page 514: 'Naval Medical Officers have, indeed, nominally acquired their rank, but are actually "a step beneath that of their brethren in the Army, and this, too, in what is called the "Senior Service,"...'

555 *If you want peace, prepare for war.* It is the motto of the Royal Navy.

Bibliography

Alison, A., *History of Europe from the Commencement of the French Revolution in MDCCLXXXIX to the restoration of the Bourbons in MDCCCXV, Volume IV* (1855) New York, Harper and Brothers; *Volume the Eleventh* (1847) Edinburgh, William Blackwood and Sons; and *Volume IX* (1841) Paris, Baudry's European Library.

Allen, J., *The Life of Lord Viscount Nelson, Duke of Bronte etc* (1853) London, George Routledge.

Allen, J., *Battles of the British Navy Vol II* (1852) London, Henry G. Bohn.

Andrews, C., *The Prisoners' Memoirs: Or, Dartmoor Prison etc* (1852) New York, (author).

Armstrong, J., *Notices of the War of 1812* (1836) New York, George Dearborn.

Auchinleck, G., *A History of the War Between Great Britain and the United States of America during the years 1812, 1813, and 1814* (1855) Toronto, Maclear and Co.

Bancroft, E.N., *An Essay on the Disease called Yellow Fever etc* (1821) Baltimore, Cushing and Jewett.

Barker, M.H., *The Life of Nelson etc* (1836) London, Frederic Shoberl.

Beamish, R., *Memoir of the Life of Sir Marc Isambard Brunel etc* (1862) London, Longman & Co.

Beatty, W., *Authentic Narrative of the Death of Lord Nelson etc (*1807) London, T. Davison.

Bell, J., *Bells' British Theatre - Tragedies Vol VII* (1780) London, (for author).

Bent, S.A., *Familiar Short Sayings of Great Men etc* (1887) Boston, Ticknor and Company.

Bentham, M.S., *The Life of Brigadier-General Sir Samuel Bentham etc* (1862) London, Longman & Co.

Biddle, C., *Autobiography of Charles Biddle etc* (1883) Philadelphia, E. Claxton and Company.

BIBLIOGRAPHY

Bigland, J., *A Sketch of the History of Europe, from the Year 1783 to the General Peace in 1814 etc Vol I* (1815) Longman & Co.

Bissett, R., *The History of the Reign of George III to the Termination of the Late War, Vol VI* (1803) London, T.N. Longman and O. Rees.

Bourrienne, Louis Antoine Fauvelet de, *The Life of Napoleon Bonaparte* (1832) Philadelphia, Carey and Lea.

Bourienne (de)., *Memoirs of Napoleon Bonaparte Vol III* (1885) New York, Scribner and Welford.

Bowditch, N., *The New American Practical Navigator, etc* (1807) Newburyport, Edmund M. Blunt.

Brewster, D. and Ferguson, J., *Lectures on Select Subjects etc Vol II* (1823) Edinburgh, Stirling and Slade.

Brewer, E.C., *Dictionary of Phrase and Fable etc* (1895) London, Cassell.

Briggs, R., *The English Art of Cookery etc* (1788) London, G.G.J. and J. Robinson.

Bright, J.F., *A History of England - Constitutional Monarchy* (1837) New York, E.P. Dutton and Company.

Brighton, J.G., Admiral Sir P.B.V. Broke etc (1866) London, Sampson Low and Son.

Britton, J. and Brayley, E.W., *The Beauties of England and Wales, or, Delineations, Topographical, Historical and Descriptive Vol IV* (1803) London, Thomas Maiden.

Buck, C., *Anecdotes, Religious, Moral, and Entertaining etc Vol II* (1805) London, Knight and Compton.

Burke, E., *The Annual Register, or a View of the History, Politics and Literature for the Year 1758* (1795) London, J. Dodsley; and *for the Year 1803* (1805) London, W. Otridge and others.

Burnham, S.M., *Struggles of the Nations, or The Principal Wars, Battles, Sieges, and Treaties of the World Vol II* (1891) Boston, Lee and Shepard.

Butler, F., *Sketches of Universal History etc* (1819) Hartford, Cooke & Hale.

Campbell, J., *Naval History of Great Britain etc Vol VIII* (1813) London, John Stockdale.

Campbell, J., Berkenhout (Dr.), Yorke, H.R., Stevenson, W., *Lives of the British Admirals etc Vol VIII* (1817) London, J. Harris.

Cannon R., *The Thirty-First, or The Huntingdonshire Regiment of Foot* (1850) London, W. Clowes and Sons.

Cary, J., *Cary's New Itinerary, or, an accurate delineation of the great roads etc* (1802) London (for author).

Carey, M., *The Olive Branch: or, Faults on Both sides etc* (1815) Philadelphia, by the author.

Chambers, R. (ed), *A Biographical Dictionary of Eminent Scotsmen etc Vol I* (1872) London, Blackie.

Charnock, J., *Biographia navalis etc Vol V* (1797) London, R. Faulder.

Charnock, J., *Biographical Memoirs of Lord Viscount Nelson etc* (1806) London, H.D. Symonds.

Clark, M., *Sketches of the Naval History of the United States etc* (1813) Philadelphia, M. Carey.

Clarkson, T. (Rev), *An Essay On The Impolicy of The African Slave Trade, Second Part* (1788) London, J. Phillips.

Clerk, J., *An Essay on Naval Tactics, Systematical and Historical etc* (1804) Edinburgh, Archibald Constable & Co.

Collins, A., *Collins's Peerage of England; Genealogical, Biographical, and Historical Vol V* (1812) London, various.

Coote, C., *The History of Europe from the Peace of Amiens, in 1802, to Pacification of Paris, in 1815* (1817) London, F.C. and J. Rivington and others.

Cowgill, J., *An Historical Account of the Luddites of 1811, 1812, and 1813 etc* (1862) Huddersfield, John Cowgill.

Craik, G.L., and MacFarlane, C., *The Pictorial History of England Vol VIII* (1849) London, Charles Knight.

Creighton, C., *A History of Epidemics in Britain, Vol II* (1894) Cambridge University Press.

Dalgleish, W.S., *Great Britain and Ireland 1689-1887* (1892) London, T. Nelson and Sons.

Dawson, L.S. (Capt), *Memoirs of Hydrography etc Part 1 - 1750 to 1830* (1830) Eastbourne, Henry W. Keay.

Deane, H.B., *The Law of Blockade: it's history, present condition, and probable future etc* (1870) London, Longmans, Green, Reader, and Dyer.

Debrett, J., *The Parliamentary Register, or, History of the proceedings and debates of the House of Commons Vol XIV* (1801).

Derrick, C., *Memoirs of the Rise and Progress of the Royal Navy* (1806) London, Black and Parry.

Dibdin, C., *The Lass That Loves A Sailor* (1811) London, by the author.

Dickens, C., *All The Year Round, a weekly journal etc Vol I* (1869) London, Chapman and Hall.

Duncan, A., *Miscellaneous Essays, Naval, Political, and Divine* (1799) London, (for the editor).

BIBLIOGRAPHY

Eardley-Wilmot, J.E. (sir), *Lord Brougham's Law Reforms etc* (1860) London, Longman & Co.

Ekins, C., *Naval Battles from 1744 to the Peace in 1844* (1824) London, Baldwin, Cradock, and Joy.

Emott, J., *Speech of the Hon. James Emott, in the House of Representatives of the United States etc* (1813) New York, J. Seymour.

Erskine May, T., *The Constitutional History of England, since the Accession of George the Third etc Vol III* (1878) London, Longmans, Green, and Co.

Falconer, W., *The Shipwreck, a poem* (1803) Edinburgh, Adam and Charles Black.

Fielding, J., *The European Magazine and London Review etc Vol 42* (1802) London, J. Sewell.

Fincham, J., *A History of Naval Architecture etc* (1851) London, Whittaker and Co.

Gander, J., *The Glory of Her Sacred Majesty Queen Anne, in the Royal Navy, and Her Absolute Sovereignty as Empress of the Sea etc* (1703) London, for the author.

Gilbert, C.S., *An Historical Survey of the County of Cornwall etc Vol I* (1817) Plymouth - Dock, J. Congdon.

Gilly, W.O.S., *Narratives of Shipwrecks of the Royal Navy between 1793 and 1857 etc* (1857) London, John W. Parker.

Goldsmith, O., *History of England etc* (1823) London, G. and W.B. Whittaker.

Gourly, J., *On the Great Evils of Impressment and its Mischievous Effects in the Royal Navy and the Merchant Service etc* (1838) Southampton, John Wheeler.

Granville, G., *A Companion to the Plymouth and Devonport National Breakwater etc* (1825) London, Longman & Co.

Griffiths R., and G.E., *The Monthly Review, or Literary Journal etc Vol XXXVII* (1802) London, R. Griffiths.

Hamilton, W. (Sir), *The Collection of Autograph Letters and Historical Documents etc The Hamilton and Nelson Papers Vol II* (1894) private circulation.

Hampstead, J., *A Treatise on Naval Tactics, containing a new and easy mode, whereby every evolution that can be performed by fleets at sea etc* (1808) London, G. Kearsley.

Hansard, T.C., *The Parliamentary Debates from 1803 to the Present Time etc Vol VII* (1812) HMSO; and *Vol XIII* (1812).

Hannay, D., *Admiral Blake* (1886) London, Longmans, Green, and Co.

Homans, J.S. (ed), *A Cyclopedia of Commerce and Commercial Navigation* (1859) New York, Harper & Brothers.

Hoste, P., *L'art des armées navales, ou traite des* évolutions *navales* (1697) Lyon, Anisson et Posuel.

Hoxland, E., *The Plymouth Dock Guide, or An Authentic Account of The Rise and Progress of that Town with the Dockyard etc* (1796) London, E. Hoxland.

Irving, W., *The Analectic Magazine* (1813) Philadelphia, M. Thomas.

James, W., *A Full and Correct Account of the Chief Naval Occurrences of the Late War between Great Britain and the United States of America etc* (1817) London, T. Egerton.

James, W., *The Naval History of Great Britain etc Vol III* (1826) London, Harding, Lepard, and Co;

Vol IV (1824) Baldwin, Cradock, and Joy; *Vol V* (1886) Richard Bentley & Son; and *Vol VI* (1836) Bentley.

Johnson, T.B., *An Impartial History of Europe etc Vol IV* (1813) London, Sherwood, Neely, and Jones.

Kimball, H., *American Naval Battles etc* (1836) Boston, J.J. Smith.

Lake, R., *Handbook of Diseases of the Ear for the use of students and practitioners* (1805) New York, William Wood and Company.

Lemprière, J., *Universal Biography etc* (1808) London, T. Cadell and W. Davies.

Lossing, B.J., *Pictorial Field-book of the War of 1812 etc* (1869) New York, Harper.

Lovell, W.S., *Personal Narrative of Events from 1799 to 1815* (1879) London, Allen.

Low, C.R., *The Great Battles of the British Navy* (1872) London, Routledge.

MacFarlane, C., *The Comprehensive History of England etc Vol IV* (1861) London, Blackie.

Maclay, E.S., *A History of the United States Navy from 1775 to 1893 Vol I* (1894) New York, Appleton.

Mahan, A.T., *The Influence of Sea Power upon the French Revolution and Empire 1793-1812* (1902) Boston, Little, Brown, and Company.

Marryat, J., *More Thoughts Still, on the state of the West Indies Colonies etc* (1818) London, Hughes & Baynes.

Massey, W.N., *A History of England during the Reign of George the Third Vol IV* (1865) London, Longmans, Green, and Co.

BIBLIOGRAPHY

Mayhew, H., *The Criminal Prisons of London and Scenes of Prison Life* (1862) London, Griffin, Bohn, and Company.

McClintock, J.N., *The Granite Monthly, Volume Four* (1881) Concord (for author).

Moore, J.J., *The British Mariner's Vocabulary* (1801) London, Hurst.

Newcomb, H. (Rev), *Cyclopedia of Missions etc* (1860) New York, Charles Scribner.

Newnham Collingwood, G.L., *A Selection from the Public and Private Correspondence of Vice-Admiral Lord Collingwood etc Vol I* (1828) London, James Ridgway.

O'Bryen, C., *Naval Evolutions, or A System of Sea-Discipline extracted from The Celebrated treatise of P. L'Hoste etc* (1762) London, W. Johnston.

Oldschool, O., *The Portfolio Vol II* (1802) Philadelphia, H. Maxwell.

Page, J.L.W., *The Coasts of Devon and Lundy Island etc* (1895) London, Horace Cox.

Paine, T., *A Letter to The English People, on the Invasion of England* (1817) London, W.T. Sherwin.

Palmer, T.H. (ed), *The Historical Register of the United States Part II* (1814) Philadelphia, G. Palmer.

Park, R., *The Art of Sea-Fighting* (1706) London, Rich. Mount and Tho. Page.

Pettigrew, T.J., *Memoirs of the life of Vice-Admiral Lord Nelson Vol I* (1849) London, T. and W. Boone.

Phillips, R., *Public Characters of 1806* (1806) London, printed for author.

Pickering, D., *The Statutes at Large etc Vol XLIV* (1804) Cambridge, R. Watts.

'Piomingo', *The Savage* (1810) Philadelphia, Thomas S. Manning.

Playfair, J., *The Works of John Playfair etc Vol III* (1822) Edinburgh, Constable.

Preble, G.H., *A Chronological History of the Origin and Development of Steam Navigation* (1895) Philadelphia, Hamersly.

Robinson, G. and J., *The Field of Mars, being an alphabetical digestion of the principal Naval and Military engagements etc Vol II* (1801) London, printed for authors.

Rockwell, C., *Sketches of Foreign travel and Life at Sea, including a cruise on board a man of war etc Vol I* (1842) Boston, Tappan and Dennett.

Roger, C., *The Rise of Canada: From Barbarism to Wealth and Civilization Vol I* (1856) Quebec, Peter Sinclair.

Roosevelt, T., *The Naval War of 1812 etc* (1882) New York, G.P. Putnam's Sons.

Rose, J.H., *The Revolutionary and Napoleonic Era, 1789-1815* (1834) London, C.J. Clay and Sons.

Savage, J., *Some Account of New Zealand, Particularly the Bay of Islands etc* (1807) London, Murray.

Scott, W., (Sir) *The Life of Napoleon the Great, Emperor of the French* (1887) Philadelphia, Lippincott.

Sherburne, A., *Memoirs of Andrew Sherburne: a Pensioner of the Navy of the Revolution* (1831) Providence, H.H. Brown.

Shippen, E., *Naval Battles of The World; Great Decisive Contests On The Sea etc* (1894) Toronto, C.R. Parish.

Slush, B., *The Navy Royal, or a sea-cook turned projector etc* (1709) London, Bragge.

Smith, T., (Rev) and Choules, J.O. (Rev), *The Origins and History of Missions etc Vol 1* (1832) Boston, S. Walker and Lincoln & Edmands.

Smyth, W.H., *The Sailor's Word-Book etc* (1867) London, Blackie.

Smollett, T., *The Critical Review; Or, Annals of Literature by A Society of Gentlemen Vol IX* (1794); *Vol XXXIII* (1801); and *XXXIV* (1802), London, S. Hamilton.

Southey, R., *Life of Nelson* (1892) London, Macmillan.

Southey, R., *The Complete Poetical Works of William Cowper* (1849) London, Henry G. Bohn.

Southey, T., *Chronological History of the West Indies Vol III* (1827) London, Longman & Co.

Steel, D., *Ship-Master's Assistant and Owner's Manual etc* (1790) London (by the author).

Steel, P., *Observations and Instructions for the use of the commissioned, the junior, and other officers of the Royal Navy etc* (1804) London (for author).

Steel, P., *Steel's Naval Chronologist, of the Late War From its Commencement in February 1793, to its Conclusion in 1801 etc.* (1806) London, Steel.

Stephen J., *New Reasons for Abolishing The Slave Trade etc* (1807) London, Butterworth.

Stephen, L., *Dictionary of National Biography Vol XIII* (1888) London, Smith, Elder & Co.

Stephens, H.M., *A History of the French Revolution Vol II* (1891) New York, Charles Scribner's Sons.

Taine, H.A., *The Origins of Contemporary France: The French Revolution Vol III* (1885) New York, Henry Holt and Company.

BIBLIOGRAPHY

Thiers, L.A., *History of the Consulate and the Empire of France under Napoleon Vol II* (1893) Philadelphia, Lippincott.

Tooke, T., *Thoughts and Details on the High Prices of the Last Thirty Years, Part One* (1823) London, John Murray.

Toynbee, A., *Lectures on the Industrial Revolution of the 18th Century in England* (1887) London, Rivingtons.

Trotter, T., *A Practical Plan for manning the Royal Navy etc* (1819) Newcastle, Longman & Co.

Tuckey, J.H., *Maritime Geography and Statistics, or A Description of the Ocean and its Coasts etc Vols I and II* (1815) London, Black, Parry and Co.

Turnor, H., *Astra Castra, Experiments and Adventures in the atmosphere* (1865) London, Chapman and Hall.

Urban, S., *The Gentleman's Magazine and Historical Chronicle etc, Vols LXI* (1791), *LXVII* (1797), *LXXI* (1801), *LXXV* (1802), *LXXV* (1804), *LXXII* (1805), *LXXVII* (1807) London, John Nichols and Son, and *Vol LXXXIV* (1814) London, Nichols, Son, and Bentley.

Walker, A., *The Life of Andrew Jackson etc* (1890) Philadelphia, Keystone.

Walsh, R., *An Appeal From the Judgments of Great Britain etc* (1819) Philadelphia, Mitchell, Ames, and White.

Wanostrocht, V., *The British Constitution or an Epitome of Blackstone's Commentaries on the Laws of England, for the use of schools* (1823) London, Longman & Co.

Ward, N., *A Complete and Humorous Account of all the Remarkable Clubs and Societies in the Cities of London and Westminster etc* (1756) London, J. Wren.

Warner, R., *A Tour Through Cornwall in the Autumn of 1808* (1809) Bath, Richard Cruttwell.

Watts, J., *Life of William Pitt late Prime Minister of Great Britain etc* (1806) Philadelphia, Manning.

Webster, N., *Miscellaneous Papers on Political and Commercial Subjects* (1802) New York, Belden.

Wilberforce, W., *A Letter on The Abolition of the Slave Trade etc* (1807) London, Cadell.

Wilkinson, J., *Tutamen Nauticum: or, the Seaman's Preservation etc* (1764) London, Dodsley.

Worsley, W., *Trafalgaris Pugna; the Battle of Trafalgar etc* (1808) Bath, Wood and Cunningham.

Young, T., *A Course of Lectures on Natural Philosophy and the Mechanical Arts etc Vol I* (1807) London, Joseph Johnson.

Zimmermann, W., *A Popular History of Germany: from the Earliest Period to the Present Day Vol IV* (1878) New York, Henry J. Johnson.

Journals, Articles, Reports etc by Unknown Authors

Abstracts of the British Navy; showing how it stood, in ships, tons and classification, at the commencement of every year, from 1793 inclusive (1821).

A Collection of State Papers relative to the War against France etc Vol VII (1799) London, J. Debrett.

A Compendious Abstract of the Public General Acts etc Vol XVIII (1840) London, E.B. Ince.

A Dictionary, geographical, statistical, and historical Vol I (1854) London, Longman & Co.

A Military and Naval Encyclopaedia etc (1879) Headquarters, Eight Infantry, US Army.

An Analytical Index to the Sixteen Volumes of the First Series of the Repertory of the Arts and Manufactures etc (1806) London, John Wyatt.

An Answer to Mr. Pitt's Attack upon Earl St. Vincent and the Admiralty in His Motion etc (1804) London, Henry Ebers.

An Enquiry into the present state of the British Navy etc by an Englishman (1815) London, W. McDowell.

An Essay on Signals. By an officer of the British Navy (1788) London, Stafford and Davenport.

A New Canting Dictionary: Comprehending all the Terms, Ancient and Modern, used in the several tribes etc (1725) London, 'Booksellers of London'.

Annual Report of the Poor Law Commissioners for England and Wales (1844) London, HMSO.

Blackwood's Edinburgh Magazine Vol XVIII (1825) Edinburgh, William Blackwood.

Brett's Illustrated Naval History of Great Britain etc (1871) London, Publishing Office.

Cobbett's Annual Register Vol IV (1803) London, Cox and Baylis.

Cobbett's Complete Collection of State Trials etc Vol XXVI (1819) London, Hansard.

Cobbett's Parliamentary Debates Vol III etc (1805) Brettell, *Vol VIII etc* (1807) Hansard, *Vol X etc* (1808) Brettell, *Vol IV etc* (1812) Longman, *Vol XXI etc* (1812) Hansard.

Cobbett's Political Register Vol VII (1806) Cox and Baylis, *Vol XXII* (1812) for the author, *Vol XXIV* (1813) for the author, and *Vol XXXIV* (1819) Dolby.

Encyclopaedia Britannica etc *Vol III* (1797) and *Vol 16* (1810) Edinburgh, Bell and Macfarquhar.

General Index to British and Foreign State Papers Vol 1 to Vol XLII 1373-1853, Vol XLII (1865) London, William Ridgway.

Harper's New Monthly Magazine Vol XXIV (1862) New York, Harper.

Instructions for the Conducting of Ships of War, explanatory of, and relative to, the Signals contained in the Signal-book herewith delivered (1800) London.

Journals of the Society of Arts No. 731, Vol XV (1866) London, Bell.

Journals of the House of Commons etc (1810) London, House of Commons.

Manuscript Transmitted from St. Helena By An Unknown Channel (1817) London, John Murray.

Pantologia, A New Cyclopaedia etc Vols II and *XI* (1813) London, various.

Papers Presented to Parliament in 1809 (1809) London, A. Strahan.

Papers Relative to the Discussion with Spain in 1802, 1803, and 1804, (1805) London, James Ridgway.

Parliamentary abstracts, containing the substance of all important papers laid before the two Houses of Parliament etc (1826) London, Longman & Co.

Proceedings of the First Twenty Years of the Religious Tract Society, etc (1820) London, Benjamin Bensley.

Regulations and Instructions Relating to His Majesty's Service at Sea (1787) London, printer unknown, and (1808) London, W. Winchester and Son.

Remarks on the Present Condition of the Navy, And particularly of the Victualling (1700) London, unknown.

Scientific American (1894) New York, Munn and Co.

Select Reviews of Literature, and Spirit of Foreign Magazines Vol VII (1812) Philadelphia, John F. Watson.

Signal-book for the Ships of War (1799) Madras, Henry Edles.

Statement Respecting The Prevalence of Certain Immoral Practices in His Majesty's Navy (1821) London, Ellerton and Henderson.

The Annual Register, or a View of the History, Politics and Literature for the Year 1793 (1797) London, Dodsley; *for the Year 1801* (1802) Rivington; *for the Year 1802* (1802) Rivington; *for the Year 1806* (1806) Rivington; *for the Year 1805* (1807) Otridge; *for the Year 1807* (1809) Otridge; *for the Year 1808* (1809) Otridge; *for the Year 1814* (1815) Otridge; *for the Year 1817* (1818) Baldwin, Cradock, and Joy; and *for the Year 1833* (1834) Baldwin and Cradock.

The Atheneum; or, Spirit of the English Magazines etc Vol II (1825) Boston, Munroe and Francis.

The Book of Common Prayer etc (1743) Cambridge, Bentham.

The British Chronologist etc Vol III (1775) London, Kearsley.

The British Review, and the London Critical Journal Vol X (1817) London, Baldwin, Cradock, and Joy.

The British Navy Triumphant! Being copies of the London Gazettes Extraordinary etc (1805) Oxford, J. Cooke, J. Parker, R. Bliss, and R. Bliss.

The Christmas Tribute and New Year's Gift, a souvenir for MDCCCLL (1851) Philadelphia, Butler.

The Economic Review etc Vol IV (1894) London, Rivington, Percival & Co.

The Edinburgh Annual Register for 1815 (1817) and *for 1817 Vol X* (1821) Edinburgh, Constable and Co.

The Edinburgh Medical and Surgical Journal etc Volume Ninth (1813) Edinburgh, Constable.

The Edinburgh Review, or Critical Journal Vol XX (1812) Edinburgh, Constable.

The European Magazine and London Review etc Vol 42 (1802), *Vol 46* (1804), *Vol 50* (1806) London (for the proprietors), and *Vol 71* (1817) London, James Aspern.

The Lady's Magazine etc Vol XIII (1782) London, G. Robinson.

The Literary Panorama, being a review of books, magazine of varieties, and Annual Register etc Vol VII and *Vol IV* (1807) London, Cox, Son, and Baylis.

The London Gazette for the Year 1849 Vol I (1849) London, Harrison and Son.

The Mechanics Magazine etc Vol XLVIII (1848) London, Robertson and Co.

The Medical Times: A Journal of Medical and Chemical Science etc Volume The Nineteenth, October 14th 1848 to July 30th 1849 (1849) London, Orr and Co.

The Monthly Anthology and Boston Review etc Vol X (1811) Boston, T.B. Wait and Co.

The Monthly Magazine, or British Register (1815) London, Becket and Porter.

The Monthly Magazine, or Literary Journal Enlarged etc Vol LXXVII (1803) London, Richard Phillips.

The Monthly Review, or Literary Journal etc Vols XXXVII (1767), *XXXIV* (1801), and *XL* (1803) London, R. Griffiths, and *Vol LXXIV* (1814) London, Becket and Porter.

The Naval Chronicle Vols II (1799) and *IV* (1801) London, Joyce Gold; *Vol VI* (1801) London, Burney and Gold; and *Vols IX* (1803), *XIV* (1805), *XV* (1806), *XVII* (1807), *XIX* (1808), *XXVII* (1812) and *XXXIV* (1815) London, Joyce Gold.

The New American Cyclopaedia etc Vol XIV (1869) New York, Appleton and Co.

The Parliamentary Debates Vol III for 1803 (1805), *Vol VII for 1806 etc* (1812) Longman, and *Vol XXIV etc* (1813) Hansard.

The Picture of Plymouth being a correct guide to the public establishments etc (1812) Plymouth, Rees and Curtis.

The Popular Encyclopaedia Vol IX (1817) London, Blackie.

The Popular Science Monthly Vol III (1876) New York, Appleton.

The Quarterly Review Vol XII (1815) London, John Murray.

The Sailor's Magazine and Naval Journal Vol V (1832) New York (published by the society).

The Scots Magazine and Edinburgh Literary Miscellany for 1805 etc Vol LXVII (1805) Edinburgh, Constable; and *for February 1810 etc Vol LXXII* (1810) Edinburgh, Harden.

The Southern Review Vol V (1830) Charleston, A.E. Miller.

The Statutes at Large from the Thirtieth Year of the Reign of King George III etc (1794) London, Charles Eyre and Andrew Strahan.

The Tourist's Companion, being a guide to the towns of Plymouth, Plymouth-Dock, Stonehouse, Morice-Town, Stoke etc (1823) London, Longman & Co.

The Western Antiquary; or, Devon and Cornwall Notebook Vol I (1882) Plymouth, Latimer & Son.

The Wooden World Dissected (1802) London, unknown.

Voyage Around The World in the years 1803, 1804, 1805, and 1806 etc Vol I (1813) London, John Murray.

Index

The words Britain, British, England, fleet, France, French, Great Britain, navy and squadron appear regularly, so are not included in this index. Neither are canting crew words.

INDEX

INDEX

INDEX

INDEX

INDEX

INDEX